Barron Field's
MEMOIRS OF WORDSWORTH

Barron Field's
MEMOIRS OF WORDSWORTH

Edited by

GEOFFREY LITTLE

SYDNEY UNIVERSITY PRESS
for AUSTRALIAN ACADEMY OF THE HUMANITIES

Monograph 3

SYDNEY UNIVERSITY PRESS
Press Building, University of Sydney

UNITED KINGDOM, EUROPE, MIDDLE EAST, AFRICA, CARIBBEAN
Prentice/Hall International, International Book Distributors Ltd
Hemel Hempstead, England
NORTH AND SOUTH AMERICA
ISBS Division, Blackwell North America, Inc., Portland, Oregon

National Library of Australia Cataloguing-in-Publication data:

Field, Barron, 1786-1846.
    Barron Field's memoirs of Wordsworth/edited by
    Geoffrey Little.—Sydney: Sydney University Press
    for the Australian Academy of the Humanities, 1975.—
    (Australian Academy of the Humanities, Monograph; 3).
    Contains condensed version of the unpublished 'Memoirs
    of the life and poetry of William Wordsworth' by Barron
    Field with two letters from Field to Wordsworth.
    ISBN 0 424 00012 1.

    1. Wordsworth, William, 1770-1850—Criticism and inter-
    pretation. I. Little, Geoffrey, ed. II. Title. III. Title:
    Memoirs of the life and poetry of William Wordsworth.
    (Series).

821.7

First published 1975
© Geoffrey Little 1975 Introduction and Notes
Printed in Australia at The Griffin Press, Adelaide

CONTENTS

INTRODUCTION

Barron Field's manuscript *Memoirs of the Life and Poetry of William Wordsworth*,[1] which bears a number of interesting notes by the poet, has been known of since Knight drew on it for his *Life* of 1889. In 1905 he published two articles in the *Academy* briefly surveying the *Memoirs* but these give only a few passages and no very full account of the work (of about half of which there are two versions); nor do they give much information about Field. Some of the Wordsworth notes omitted from Knight's *Life* have been printed in the *Times Literary Supplement*,[2] though not with complete accuracy, and several editions and studies have made passing use of the notes; but the manuscript as a whole remains unpublished. Field's sister Maria offered it to Knight in 1883 with the remark 'There were no steps taken by any of our family to publish the manuscript. This work had the sanction of Mr. Wordsworth, who had not only read it, but had made several marginal notes in the M.S.S.' (The 'sanction' is unlikely.) The manuscript was acquired by the British Museum from Sotheby's in 1926.

Field seems to have had two motives for writing the *Memoirs*: first, to defend a long-admired friend from charges and criticisms made over the years and to ensure his full recognition; and then, when Wordsworth discouraged immediate publication because defence was no longer needed and he disliked its 'personally disagreeable' elements, to be first with a full critical biography after his death. As it happened Field, the younger by sixteen years, died first.

As little is conveniently on record about Field's literary life and activities I begin with a brief biography[3] and an account of his correspondence with and about Wordsworth. Two of Field's unpublished

---

[1] BM MS Add. 41325-7 (includes Maria L. Field's letters to Knight of 5 and 10 December 1883).

[2] *Life of William Wordsworth*, 3 vols, Edinburgh 1889; 'A Literary Causerie', *The Academy*, LXIX (1905), pp. 1332-4, 1358-61; R. Sencourt, 'Wordsworth', correspondence, *Times Literary Supplement*, 28 April 1950, p. 261.

[3] Besides the sources noted I have consulted *Australian Dictionary of Biography* (*ADB*); *Dictionary of National Biography* (*DNB*); J. V. Byrnes, 'Barron Field—Recultivated', *Southerly*, XXI (1961), pt 3 pp. 6-18; *Leigh Hunt's Autobiography*, ed. J. E. Morpurgo, London 1949; E. Blunden, *Leigh Hunt's 'Examiner' Examined* and *Leigh Hunt*, London 1928 and 1930; and E. V. Lucas, *Life of Charles Lamb*, 2 vols, London 1921.

letters are given in an Appendix; these and other letters show how seriously Wordsworth took his admirer's criticism. My chief purpose however is to make available the *Memoirs*, with some of Field's long-windedness deflated, and the marginal notes.

Field was born on 23 October 1786 and died on 11 April 1846. He was at Christ's Hospital with Leigh Hunt, a few years after Lamb and Coleridge. Later he became particularly close to Hunt, writing for him and offering help during his imprisonment. He was the 'B.F.' of Lamb's famous visit in 1815 to 'Mackery End, in Hertfordshire', published six years later with the hope that 'peradventure he shall read this on the far distant shores where the Kangaroo haunts', and the subject of 'Distant Correspondents', 1822, based on a personal letter to Field of 1817. Field was a regular visitor to Lamb's Wednesday or Thursday evening gatherings in 1815. He attended Talfourd's last dinner party for Lamb in 1834 and wrote a long and affectionate obituary notice. Field also wrote an obituary for Coleridge, whom he seems to have known quite well, visiting him in 1813 and 1814 (when the Shakespeare notes mentioned below may have been written) and again in 1824 and 1825. And of course he knew Crabb Robinson, Collier, Talfourd, Barnes, and others of that circle, which sometimes met at his rooms at 4 Hare Court, the Temple.

Field was entered on the books of the Inner Temple in 1809 and called to the Bar in 1814. In 1816 he was appointed Judge of the Supreme Court of Civil Judicature of New South Wales, taking up the post in February 1817. Field administered 'tedious justice in inauspicious unliterary Thiefland' (as Lamb put it in a review of his first Australian poems in the *Examiner* of 16 January 1820) until February 1824, becoming involved in the colony's social reforms and its legal development. Some of his actions (they are discussed in some detail in *ADB*) were strongly criticized.

Just before Field, then newly-married, set sail, Hunt wrote for him an occasional poem beginning, 'Dear Field, my old friend, who love straightforward verse, And will take it, like marriage, for better, for worse . . .' In October 1824, soon after his return, an 'Epistle to B- F- Esq., in Imitation of Pope', signed 'H', appeared in the *New Monthly Magazine*. It was bitter about the changes in London. About this time Crabb Robinson noted that Field 'talks amusingly, although there is something of grand ha! about him'. Their earlier acquaintance was renewed and in 1828 they walked together to see Mrs Blake, Field buying a proof of a Blake engraving.[4]

[4] *Blake, Coleridge, Wordsworth, Lamb . . . the Remains of Henry Crabb Robinson*, ed. E. J. Morley, Manchester and London 1922, p. 84; *Henry Crabb Robinson on Books and their Writers*, ed. Morley, 3 vols, London, 1938, I, pp. 315, 353.

Field practised in England, living in Liverpool, until 1829. Then, after an offer in 1828 to be advocate fiscal in Ceylon,[5] he was appointed first as a judge and then as Chief Justice of Gibraltar. He held the post until 1841, corresponding with friends regularly, before settling in the south of England.

When first at the Inner Temple, Field contributed dramatic criticism to the *Times*, encouraged Leigh Hunt to review for it, and was influential in Barnes's appointment. In 1810 he had an article in the *Quarterly Review* on Nott's edition of Herrick. In 1811 he produced an edition of *Blackstone's Commentaries* which was frequently reprinted, and various legal papers followed. He published poems in Hunt's *Examiner* in 1811, 1812, 1815 and 1816, and collaborated in his short-lived *Reflector* in 1811-12. The *Dictionary of National Biography* notes that Field's prose pieces were signed with three daggers: thus he contributed a 'Shakespeare Sermon' to the first number of the *Reflector*; a dialogue concerning the 'Pruriencies of our Old Poets' (prompted by Chalmers' new *English Poets*) and essays on 'What Constitutes a Madman?' and the 'Effects of Wealth' to the second number; a 'Character of an Exaggerator' to the fourth (and last) number; and communications from 'The Law Student' to the first, second and third numbers. His writing here, perhaps influenced by Hunt and Lamb, is often sharp and lively—unfortunately unlike that of much of the *Memoirs*.

At some time Field may have contemplated an edition of Shakespeare. There is in the Library of New South Wales a twenty-one-volume Shakespeare, the 1803 printing of Isaac Reid's 1778 edition, which has detailed textual and critical notes by Field as well as notes apparently by Hunt, John Milford, and Coleridge.

In Sydney in 1819 Field published two poems as *First Fruits of Australian Poetry*. To open the volume he adapted (with acknowledgement) Joseph Hall's Prologue to *Vergidemiarum*, Book I, ll. 3-4, in order to claim jokingly (but mistakenly) to be the colony's first poet:

> I first adventure. Follow me who list;
> And be the second Austral Harmonist.

Some readers have taken Field's claim too solemnly, at the same time overlooking the minor virtues of the poems themselves.[6] Lamb's review, tongue in cheek, compared 'Kangaroo' to Marvell's 'Bermudas' and commended the 'dawn of refinement' at Sydney. In a letter of

[5] *DNB* errs (following the *Gentleman's Magazine*, 1846, Pt I, p. 646) in implying that Field was offered Ceylon before he went to New South Wales.
[6] See Byrnes, 'Barron Field . . . ', and Bernard Smith, *European Vision and the South Pacific*, Oxford 1960, for reasonable brief discussions of the poems.

16 August 1820 he assured Field that Wordsworth, Coleridge and Charles Lloyd were 'hugely taken' with the poem.[7] Field then published two poems in the new *Australian Magazine*, in 1821 and 1823, and two in the *Gazette*, in March 1822. Of these all but the first (the weakest) were added to the second edition of *First Fruits*, 1823, together with a rather good poem, 'On Reading the Controversy between Lord Byron and Mr. Bowles'.

The *Memoirs of James Hardy Vaux*, a significant piece of rogue writing, was written in 1815. Field edited the manuscript, possibly taking the opportunity to bowdlerize it,[8] contributed a Prefatory Advertisement dated May 1817, and persuaded Murray to publish it in 1819. He probably also had a hand in the editions of 1827 and 1829 after his return to England.

In Sydney Field also prepared two papers, 'On the Aboriginals of New Holland and Van Diemen's Land', read to the Philosophical Society in January 1822, and 'On the Rivers of New South Wales', read to the Agricultural Society in July 1823. These were later printed in *Geographical Memoirs of New South Wales*, 1825, which Field edited. He included also *First Fruits*, a 'Glossary of the Natural History of New South Wales and Van Diemen's Land', and (reprinted from the *London Magazine*) narratives of his voyages to and from the colony and accounts of his excursions within it. In the account of crossing the Blue Mountains Field mentions Wordsworth on the power of the hills, although (it has been said) he was clearly happier when he reached the flat and fertile Bathurst plains.[9]

From Gibraltar Field sent the long memoir of Coleridge in Longman's *Annual Biography and Obituary of 1834* (1835). He drew heavily on Hazlitt and on *Biographia Literaria*, and then remarked:

His poems, even when most metaphysical, are as intelligible as they are beautiful . . . . Instead of answering the repeated calls of Mr. Wordsworth and his other friends for more poetry, thus has this great genius dreamt and talked his life away, in literary projects, in extemporary lectures, in metaphysical abortions, and in universal procrastination.

Field's obituary of Lamb appeared in the *Annual Biography* for the following year.[10] He lost no time in proposing himself as Lamb's

[7] *Works of Charles and Mary Lamb*, ed. E. V. Lucas, 6 vols, London 1912, Vol. I, pp. 232-5; *Letters*, ed. Lucas, 3 vols., London, 1935, Vol. II, p. 282.
[8] The suggestion is made by Vaux's most recent editor, N. McLachlan, Melbourne 1964.
[9] See Smith, *European Vision and the South Pacific*, pp. 181-8.
[10] Only the Lamb obituary bears Field's initials but his authorship of both is clear from a letter to Crabb Robinson from Gibraltar, 16 February 1835, 'Having written the Memoir of Coleridge for Longman's last Annual Biography, I have

biographer ('I should make the next best after [Southey]'); but soon acknowledged the 'good taste and skill, with which Talfourd has erected the literary monument to our dear friend'.[11] Talfourd's Preface acknowledged Field's help along with some of 'the greatest of our living authors'.

Another volume of verse, *Spanish Sketches* (1841, reissued 1843), came out of Field's spell in Gibraltar. When he finally settled in England he edited some of Heywood for the Shakespeare Society: *King Edward IV*, Parts I and II, was published in 1842 and *The Fair Maid of the Exchange* and *Fortune by Land and Sea* (Heywood and Rowley) in 1846. Field also edited *The True Tragedy of Richard III* together with Thomas Legge's *Ricardus Tertius* for the Society, the volume appearing in 1844.

In 1841-2 Field renewed his interest in the issue of literary copyright; he wrote in the *Memoirs* (B version) that he helped Wordsworth with an article on the subject. Earlier, in 1837, he had sympathized with Talfourd's support of a Copyright Bill which would have assisted Wordsworth, and in the *Memoirs* recalled Talfourd's speeches in the House.[12]

In 1843 Field was consulted about Crabb Robinson's plan for a volume of *Reminiscences* from his 1800-5 letters for private distribution.[13] In 1844 he had in mind to

> edit a complete edition of Donne for the Percy Society. To give correct copies of such good old poets will be better than so much obscure prose and dramatic trash . . . shall preserve the poem containing the wittiest piece of bawdy in the world; not directing any body's attention to the poem; and then none but the wise (whom it will not harm) will read it, if they do.[14]

---

promised something of Lamb for the next'. This unpublished letter (noticed in Lucas, *Life of Charles Lamb*, Vol. I, p. 439, but not in *Correspondence of Crabb Robinson with the Wordsworth Circle*, ed. E. J. Morley, 2 vols, Oxford 1927), together with the published and unpublished letters to HCR quoted below, is among the letters in Dr Williams's Library. (While the Trustees have allowed access to the manuscripts they are not responsible for the selection made, and author and publisher waive any copyright in extracts so far as its exercise might debar others from using and publishing the same material.)

[11] Ibid., and letter to HCR of 16 November 1837.

[12] See Chapter II and B additions to Chapter III below, and my note 'Wordsworth . . . and the Copyright Act', *Notes and Queries*, Vol. ccx, pp. 411-13.

[13] 'I agree with you that your Letters of 1800-05 will make a most interesting typography', to HCR, 2 August 1843, from Brighton. Some of the HCR letters were printed in the *Monthly Register*; see *HCR in Germany 1800-05*, ed. E. J. Morley, London 1919, p. 177.

[14] Letters to HCR of 14 August and 21 October 1844, from Torquay. Nothing seems to have come of the plan.

Field's love for Wordsworth began in 1800 when, at fourteen, he first heard the sweet poem 'We are Seven'. He became 'through evil report and through good report, an admirer (and subsequently a friend) of the poet'. He cheered his studies with *Lyrical Ballads* and, 'at the hazard of ridicule from the whole Edinburgh-Review-blinded Bar', carried *The Excursion* on his circuit (Chapter XII). He was a devoted and assiduous critic; the evidence of the letters and the *Memoirs* shows both the closeness and care of his reading and the attention Wordsworth paid to his detailed suggestions. Field's enthusiasm made at least one important 'convert to his poetical faith, in a young heart, who is now deservedly the leader of that circuit, and author of the most beautiful tragedy of our times'. Talfourd acknowledged Field's influence in a later preface to *Ion*.

Field and Wordsworth probably first met as early as 13 May 1812 at a dinner at which the poet criticized John Wilson ('Christopher North'); Field called his work 'Wordsworth and Water'.[15] They met on 23 May 1815 at Lamb's, when Wordsworth was 'very chatty on poetry' (probably about *The Excursion*), and again on 1 June.[16] Closer acquaintance probably came later. Lamb gave Field a note of introduction in September 1824 which recalled the earlier meeting.[17] The Dedication to the *Memoirs* records that Field and Horatio Smith visited Wordsworth and Southey in the Lakes in the summer of 1827. Wordsworth visited Field in Liverpool in late March or early April 1828 and Field wrote on 10 April to thank him for his candid discussion of the revisions in the 1827 five-volume edition. After the visit, Field wrote, he marked his earlier texts, 'so as to shew the eye hereafter the various readings at a glance'. (He had already annotated and interleaved the two octavo volumes of 1815.) His exercise was 'amply repaid by both a deeper insight into the poet's meaning and a better lesson in the art of poetry, than I could have derived from any other sources'. He joked hopefully about a variorum edition, 'the *fifteenth* Edition, with notes by Barron Field'. The long letter has influential comments, general and particular. His collation led Field to detect

> a little disposition in your alterations, to mitigate that simplicity of speech, which you taught us was the true language of the heart, and to make some tardy sacrifice at the shrine of poetic diction; and thus, after having 'created the taste by which you have been enjoyed', in a small degree deserting your disciples.

[15] *Blake, Coleridge, Wordsworth, Lamb* . . . , p. 50.
[16] *HCR on Books and their Writers*, Vol. I, pp. 167, 168, and see n. 63 below.
[17] Lamb's *Letters*, Vol. II, p. 438.

Pleading his 'zealous admiration' in apology, Field criticized closely, boldly and sensibly. Wordsworth replied quite promptly and at almost equal length, probably on 24 April (apparently having first sent a note of acknowledgement). Field then wrote on 28 April offering the Wordsworths hospitality and assistance on their journey back from Cambridge to Rydal and took the opportunity to comment on Wordsworth's reply.

Wordsworth's letter, which has been printed with some errors by Knight and subsequently by de Selincourt (and with a wrong date given by Field himself in the *Memoirs*) is given in Chapter III below.[18] Field's letters of 10 and 28 April, the first of which is necessary to understand Wordsworth's letter, are in an Appendix.[19] The whole correspondence shows Field's influence.

Field wrote again on 19 December 1828 to announce his posting:

> I shall perhaps have the honour of being the first to teach your poems to the Cinnamon Groves of Ceylon .... By the bye, all your travellers 'step westward'. You have no oriental poem. I wish you would write me one, as unlike 'Lalla Rookh' as possible.

He asked about buying a copy of the Chantrey bust and praised 'The Triad' and the sonnet on 'A Gravestone . . . of Worcester Cathedral'. Wordsworth replied the next day to arrange about the bust, comment further on the two poems, and ask for a story of a Hindoo girl and her lover from Forbes's *Oriental Memoirs* as 'I should like to write a *short* India Piece'. On 24 December Field sent a different story from Forbes which he had copied from the *Quarterly Review* notice, promising to find the other in London. This was acknowledged on 19 January 1829. Field must have written again from London to tell Wordsworth of his change of destination and, probably, to send the story of the Hindoo girl, and Wordsworth replied briefly on 26 February (not dated in Knight and de Selincourt).[20] The same day Field was writing again, full of a detailed plan for Wordsworth to change his publisher to Murray, who would pay out the expenses of the five volume edition and then share equally any profits. Wordsworth's response to this busy-

---

[18] *Letters of William and Dorothy Wordsworth: The Later Years*, ed. E. de Selincourt, 3 vols, Oxford 1939, Vol. I, pp. 307-13, gives Wordsworth's reply from Knight's text; the *Memoirs*, Chapter III, gives a more accurate version. See also nn. 50, 59, 62 and 64 to the text.

[19] Field's letters to Wordsworth of 10 and 28 April 1828 and his letters mentioned below of 19 and 24 December 1828, 26 February 1829, 17 December 1836, 15 September 1837 and 21 November 1839, are in the Dove Cottage Library. I am grateful to the Trustees for permission to refer to them.

[20] For these Wordsworth letters see *Letters, Later Years*, Vol. I, pp. 340-1, 346-7, 382.

bodying has not survived but it would hardly have been sympathetic in view of Murray's failure to answer proposals put in 1825.[21]

There is a gap in the correspondence until December 1836, although from February 1835 to March 1836 Field mentioned Wordsworth three times in letters to Crabb Robinson. (In 1835 he had been dissuaded by Crabb Robinson from writing directly.) 'Oh! remember me to him!, he wrote. 'I read Wordsworth's new volume [*Yarrow Revisited*] with the purest delight ... offer to him on my part the reverential remembrances of an early and fervent disciple.' '... remember me always in the first place to Wordsworth.'[22] The last of these letters hoped for a visit; 'I cannot forego the hope of seeing not only you but the great poet, and of accompanying you to Naples and Rome'. A Tour of the Mediterranean from Wordsworth would be superior even to Samuel Rogers's *Italy*. At the end of the year, 17 December 1836, Field did write directly, regretting that illness had prevented the poet from paying 'the magnificent debt due to Naples, Florence and Rome' (cf. 'Stanzas Composed in the Simplon Pass', ll. 9, 12). He suggested Wordsworth should take a steam vessel from either Liverpool or London in the spring so that they could together visit Italy and Spain. Field praised the recent 'Yarrow Revisited' and 'On the Power of Sound' ('Never was *sound* made so much of before. Milton should have written it when blind'), although, of course, he had some 'verbal observations' to offer, along with seven mottoes for earlier poems. He nagged, 'Oh! continue the "Recluse". I wish I was Moxon. I would make you such an offer for it as would ruin me and wreck my children' (Field was childless), and mentioned Murray again. Wordsworth replied through Crabb Robinson on 28 January that 'never will I trust myself in the Atlantic in a steam boat between the Autumnal and the Vernal equinox'.[23] He did, of course, travel in Italy between March and August 1837 with Crabb Robinson, who sent to Field perhaps in consolation the long account of the tour which is in Chapter II below. Thus on 15 September Field was able to congratulate Wordsworth on his safe return, note with pleasure that some of his suggestions of the previous December had been adopted in the stereotype six-volume 1836-7 edition, and write 'I will therefore take the liberty of making a few more'. In a postscript he mentioned that a review, 'Wordsworth Stereotyped', had been sent to Wilson for *Blackwood's*; alternatively it might be given to Leigh Hunt for his *Monthly Repository*, or even to Moxon for a Preface to a volume of Wordsworth selections. The essay does not seem to have appeared,

[21] See *Letters, Later Years*, Vol. I, pp. 187-8, 197-8, 220, 221, 223.
[22] Letters to HCR of 16 February and 17 October 1835 and March 1836.
[23] *Corr. HCR*, Vol. I, p. 336 (not in *Letters, Later Years*).

although there is later a suggestion that Wordsworth received a copy.

In November 1837 Field again urged a visit, writing to Crabb Robinson:

> You positively must come next spring ... the Alhamra from its associations is a thing to interest his human taste as much as the locale of Rome. How proud I should be to house him .... Let not the scorners say that the poet went to Rome to write a Sonnet on the cuckoo .... Remember me with lyric reverence to Mr Wordsworth.[24]

In December Wordsworth told Crabb Robinson he was 'uneasy in being so long in Barron Field's debt, he having favoured me with another letter of criticism [probably that of September] upon my last Ed. Some of the remarks will be useful.'[25] A further letter to Crabb Robinson from Field on 1 March 1839 contained a 'supplementary list of verbal suggestions' to be passed to Wordsworth, with the wish that 'the great Poet would keep away from politics, and publish his Memoirs of a Tour to Italy'.[26]

Wordsworth sent a note to Field, written by Mary because of the state of his eyes, in November 1839. It was carried to Gibraltar by his nephew (John?) as a letter of introduction. Field replied on 21 November. Besides giving an account of the visit, and in a postscript suggesting three further revisions, he announced the *Memoirs* in terms which suggest the work had developed from the review mentioned in September two years before. He noted having added three introductory chapters; thus the original review would probably have started with the remark in Chapter IV:

> The poet having now taken his niche for ever in the Temple of Fame, and his foaming reviewer having subsided into a forensic judge, it may afford an useful lesson to both authors and critics, at this distance of time, to look back calmly and dispassionately upon the history of this case.

Field said that the whole had been transcribed for Moxon, though 'if you wish to strike out any passage it shall be done'. No doubt Moxon forwarded this first version of the *Memoirs*, which Wordsworth annotated before writing the discouraging letters below.

In the *Memoirs* Field states that he did not see Wordsworth from 1829 until 1840. He then stayed at Rydal Mount, probably for a short

[24] 16 November 1837. The 'Sonnet on the cuckoo' is 'The Cuckoo at Laverna', III, 218. See HCR's uncollected letter to Field quoted early in Chapter II and B addition to Chapter III.
[25] *Corr. HCR*, Vol. I, p. 350, 15 December 1837 (not in *Letters, Later Years*).
[26] Letter in part only in *Corr. HCR*, Vol. I, pp. 380-1. The *Memorials*, III, 202-9, was published in 1842.

time, during a visit to England, and later added a brief account of the visit to Chapter III. 'The poet [then] told me the story of his life, particularly of his acquaintance with Mr. Hazlitt and Mr. De Quincey, and of the several causes of the cessation of these relationships, unfit to be recorded in writing.' Wordsworth was doubtless commenting on the matter of Chapter I and nn. 13-18. He also read unpublished poems to Field and 'strolled over the "old poetic mountains"' and around Grasmere with him. Clearly Wordsworth's refusal at the beginning of the year to approve publication of the *Memoirs* had not destroyed their friendship.

Field also records that when he quitted Gibraltar in the autumn of 1841 he 'spent a few months in the neighbourhood of the poet'; and they may have met again in London in 1843.[27] Field continued to press his views of Wordsworth after this date, although eventually with reservations:

> I also thank you for your great friend's Railway Letters and Sonnets, and I wish, if he can do no better, that he would, as he says in one of his poems, 'take his last leave both of verse and prose' .... I am afraid there is a little secularity of mind in our divine poet .... he and Rydal can no more pretend to 'retirement' than the Queen. They have both bartered it for fame.

This letter to Crabb Robinson of 16 February 1845 is long and querulous.[28]

The *Memoirs* confirms the dates of composition suggested by the letters. 'The compilation of the critical portion of the following pages beguiled my leisure at Gibraltar', Field remarks in the Dedication to Horatio Smith dated 3 December 1839. At the beginning of the first chapter there is a reference to a speech of April 1838, the second chapter cites Lockhart's *Life of Scott*, 1837-8, and later there is use of Hallam's *Literature of Europe*, 1837-9, and mention of an incident in 1838. The manuscript as it stood in December 1839 was forwarded to Wordsworth, who annotated it to the end of Chapter V and no doubt read the whole. He then wrote to Moxon on 10 January 1840:

> I set my face entirely against the publication of Mr. Field's MSS .... Mr. Field has been very little in England, I imagine, for above twenty years and is consequently not aware, that much of the greatest part of his labour would only answer the purpose of reviving forgotten theories and exploded opinions. Besides, there are in his notions things that are personally *disagreeable* (not to use a harsher term) to myself and those about me. And if such an objection did not lie against the publication, it is enough that the thing is *superfluous*. In the present state of this Country in general, how

[27] *Corr. HCR*, Vol. I, p. 496.
[28] *Corr. HCR*, Vol. II, pp. 591-3, quoting 'The Two Thieves', l. 4, IV, 245.

could this kind natured Friend ever be deceived into the thought that criticism and particulars so minute could attract attention even from a few?

On 16 January he wrote to Field:

> I have at last brought myself to write to you. After maturely considering the subject, however painful it may be to me, I must regret that I am decidedly against the publication of your Critical Memoir; your wish is, I know, to serve me, and I am grateful for the strength of this feeling in your excellent heart. I am also truly proud of the pains of which you have thought my writings worthy; but I am sure that your intention to benefit me in this way would not be fulfilled. The hostility which you combat so ably is in a great measure passed away, but might in some degree be revived by your recurrence to it, so that in this respect your work would, if published, be either superfluous or injurious, so far as concerns the main portion of it. I shall endeavour, during the short remainder of my life, to profit by it, both as an author and a man, in a private way; but the notices of me by many others which you have thought it worth while to insert are full of gross mistakes, both as to facts and opinions, and the sooner they are forgotten the better. Old as I am, I live in the hope of seeing you, and should in that event have no difficulty in reconciling you to the suppression of a great part of this work entirely, and of the whole of it in its present shape . . . . One last word in matter of authorship; it is far better not to admit people so much behind the scenes, as it has been lately fashionable to do.[29]

It is interesting to notice Wordsworth's dismissal of 'forgotten theories', not to be revived, and his insistence on the privacy of the author. As to the first, some of these issues are more than ever matter for critical debate; not only Jeffrey's attacks but the central assertions of the Preface and the question of the relation between theory and practice in the poetry. As to the second, Field reproduced offensive remarks by Hazlitt about Wordsworth's character and about his attitudes to Shakespeare, Dryden, Pope and Gray (these Wordsworth called 'monstrous'). He gave a passage from De Quincey in *Tait's Magazine*, 1839, and referred to the objectionable portraits of Wordsworth and his wife and sister published in the same year. He introduced some of Coleridge's less friendly remarks, commented on his income and payment for poetry, and gave details of the Lowther lawsuit and settlement. He quoted Wordsworth's private letters to him. In the additions to Chapter III (which Wordsworth may not have seen) he mentioned Dorothy's illness.

Wordsworth's repeated reference to his age in January 1840 and his polite remarks about Field's abilities may have given Field the notion of re-writing the *Memoirs* for publication after Wordsworth's death. The annotated 1839 manuscript (which I shall call A) was perhaps

[29] *Letters, Later Years*, Vol. II, pp. 996-7, 997-8.

returned when Field stayed at Rydal Mount. It was used as a working copy for the revisions and additions which went on up to the year of Field's death. (Appendix III draws on *Blackwood's* for 1842 and 1843, an addition to Chapter II quotes from Stanley's *Life of Arnold*, 1844, and an addition to Chapter VI quotes a poem by Horace Smith, whose poetical works came out in 1846.) Field copied out the revised first six chapters (this unfinished copy will be called B) and doubtless intended to copy the whole. B absorbs most of Wordsworth's comments into the text (presumably to give the impression of close co-operation between poet and critic) and introduces fresh material most of which was drafted on A. The remainder of A similarly bears drafts of additional material.

The A manuscript itself is well padded out with long notes and extensive quotations from various poets and from earlier and contemporary criticism. (The *Memoirs* parades embarrassingly Field's wide reading, particularly in seventeenth century poetry, which goes far beyond his use of such handy compilations as Ellis's *Specimens* and Todd's monumental Milton.) There are anecdotes, many appeals to authority in the legal manner, and classical allusions and references which are often awkwardly assimilated. These practices are aggravated in B, where much of the added material is, like some of the original material, slight or irrelevant. But there are some later remarks of interest, some more severe criticisms of Wordsworth, and (despite the poet's friendly letters) more references to his private life. A number of references to him are changed to a past tense and the title 'Mr' is dropped—all signs that Field was preparing for publication after the poet's death.

Knight thought the *Memoirs* 'miscellaneous, fragmentary, gossipy, at times representative, and often egotistical. Nevertheless, they contain much interesting material, scattered among their garrulous commonplaces'.[30] This is fair, if harshly put. In general Field anticipates (and perhaps prompted) a number of Wordsworth's biographers and editors with what is now familiar information. He gives his own version of more or less important episodes and issues. In addition to items already mentioned he provides a few more lines of Wordsworth's verse, a Crabb Robinson letter, corrections to an important Wordsworth letter, parallel passages and comparisons with Gray, Pope, Crabbe, Shenstone, Akenside and others, Hartley Coleridge's comment on the Pedlar of *The Excursion* and a possible model, a full account of Wordsworth's supposed plagiarism from Landor and Quillinan's essay in defence, and other similar items of interest. Field's best critical

[30] 'A Literary Causerie', *The Academy*, p. 1132.

passages, though scattered and spilling over into cumbersome foot-notes, convey enthusiasm and discrimination. On the other hand too much of the discussion is top-heavy with quotation and goes into side tracks and seemingly random associations.

In this condensed text of the *Memoirs* I have assumed that A, the version Wordsworth read and annotated (at least up to Chapter V) is of greater interest and have followed it as far as possible. (It is not always clear when some added passages were written.) At the same time interesting passages either in or apparently intended for B have been introduced in square brackets. A good deal of trivial material has been omitted and long quotations, either verse or prose, have been identified and either omitted or condensed, in all cases with the use of the conventional elipses. Field's own omissions in quotation have been indicated by stars, and his interpolations by angle brackets.

Thus material in square brackets is either later additions (whether in A only, in B only, or in both), or editorial, as the context indicates. The latter includes identification of quotations from Wordsworth by reference to the *Poetical Works* (Ernest de Selincourt and Helen Darbishire, eds, 5 vols, rev. edn, Oxford 1952-9). *The Prose Works of William Wordsworth*, W. J. B. Owen and J. W. Smyser, eds, 3 vols, Oxford 1974, became available too late for use in this work.

Field's occasional alteration of tense or person in a quotation to fit his context has been retained (but not his inconsistent use of quotation marks). So too has his use of the text and poem numbers of 1836-7. His preferred spelling of Shakspeare's name (thus) has been made consistent. His occasional contractions have been expanded.

Field indicates sketchily most of his major sources of information and criticism (although in Chapter I he has borrowed silently a few sentences from the anonymous Memoir in Galignani's pirated 1828 *Poems*), but does not usually locate his English verse quotations. I have provided fuller references, usually to recent editions, in most cases where they may be useful, but have not identified all the classical tags.

Footnotes generally have been distinguished as follows: BF—Barron Field; WW—Wordsworth's marginal note or comment; no initial—editorial. Superscript note numbers in the text which refer to a Wordsworth marginal comment, note, letter or remark are preceded by a W, thus: ^{W98}. The Wordsworth notes themselves are printed in bold face for easy reference (but not remarks, as on p. 100, incorporated in the text). The summary headings to each chapter, repeated from the Table of Contents, have been omitted.

I would like to thank Yvonne Andrews for help with early work on the text, Robert Woof for making available some Field letters, and Jonathan Wordsworth for his hospitable encouragement of the project.

[CRITICAL] MEMOIRS OF
THE LIFE AND POETRY OF
WILLIAM WORDSWORTH,
with Extracts from his Letters to the Author,
By Barron Field, Esqr. [late] Chief Justice of Gibraltar.[1]

DEDICATION to Horatio Smith Esquire. My dear Sir, After a friendship of five and twenty years, which for the far greater part of that time a mere epistolary correspondence could keep brightly burning, to whom but you should I inscribe the following little work? To you I can say moreover, in the words of Mr Landor,

> Together we have visited the men,
> Whose song Scotch critics vainly would have drown'd.
> Ah! shall we never grasp the hand again,
> That gave the British harp its truest sound?[2]

It was in the summer of the year 1827, that you and I made that visit to Mr Wordsworth and Mr Southey at the English Lakes, and proceeded to Edinburgh, where, in the Parliament House, we were introduced to the celebrated 'Scotch critic' in question. But in that city, our love of both poetry and criticism was reconciled, at a *disjeune*[3] with the truly great and amiable Sir Walter Scott. The compilation of the critical portion of the following pages beguiled my leisure at Gibraltar. As the work is too inconsiderable for praise on the one hand, I need make no apology for these *horae juridicae subsecivae* on the

---

[1] A note at the head of page, 'Begun in 1836', apparently not in Field's hand. 'CRITICAL' in title neatly deleted, possibly in preparation for B. Beneath the title is a stanza from Cowley, 'Whoever would deposed Truth advance . . . Does to the wise a Star, to fools a Meteor, show' ('To the Royal Society', st. 8, *Poems . . . and Sundry Verses*, ed. A. R. Waller, 2 vols, Cambridge 1905-6, Vol. I, p. 452), and beneath a repeated title are some lines from William Browne, 'Well, I wot, the man that first . . . There they would begin their measure'.

[2] 'Ode to a Friend', ll. 19-22, *Poetical Works*, ed. S. Wheeler, 3 vols, London 1937, Vol. III, p. 9.

[3] Mr J. C. Maxwell suggests an allusion to *Old Mortality*, Ch. XI.

other . . . [Field here mentions a number of judges who were also men of letters] *Ego me excerpam numero*. The only honours I possess are those of being the Great poet's and your most affectionate friend, Barron Field. Gibraltar, 3rd Dec. 1839.

CONTENTS   *Chapter I*. Biography of the Poet. History of the Lyrical Ballads. Extracts from Messrs Hazlitt, Coleridge and Cottle. Enumeration of the Poet's Works. *Chapter II*. Biography of the Poet continued. Extract from Mr Serjeant Talfourd. Mr Hazlitt's Portrait of the Poet. Sir Walter Scott's. *Chapter III*. The Poet's Correspondence with the Author. Alterations of his Poems. On Similes. 'Miserrimus'. Subjects for poetry. *Chapter IV*. Biography of the Poet concluded. Poetical criticisms of the Edinburgh Review. The Rejected Addresses. Proper office of criticism. Extracts from Dryden and Addison. Mr Coleridge's Vindication of the Poet. *Chapter V*. The principles of poetry—illustrated by extracts from Sidney, Bacon, D'Avenant, and Milton, and by specimens from Wordsworth. *Chapter VI*. Principles of poetry and painting—illustrated by an extract from Opie's Lectures on Painting. Principles of poetry illustrated by extracts from Mr Wordsworth's Preface, and from Burke's Inquiry into the Sublime and Beautiful. Poetry, Painting and Music. *Chapter VII*. The principles and province of poetry concluded. Personifications. Science and Poetry. Akenside and Campbell. *Chapter VIII*. The Lyrical Ballads. Poetic Diction. Difference between the poet's theory and his practice. Extract from the Guardian. Shenstone. Crabbe. Poems by Gray and Collins. *Chapter IX*. Mr Wordsworth's theory continued. Difference between his earlier and his later editions. 'The Beggars'. *Chapter X*. Classification and detail of Mr Wordsworth's poems. Verbal criticisms, mottoes suggested and parallel passages. Elegy on the Deaths of George and Sarah Green. 'Andrew Jones'. Henry Vaughan's 'Retreat'. *Chapter XI*. The Excursion. Poetry of Lord Byron. Mr Montgomery's 'Grave'. School of Pope. School of Wordsworth. *Chapter XII*. Philosophy of Mr Wordsworth's poetry. Sir James McIntosh's opinions of the poet. The Excursion compared with the Pleasures of the Imagination. Conclusion. *Appendixes*. I. Extracts from the Reviews of the Lyrical Ballads. II. Extracts from Mr Wordsworth's pamphlet on the Convention of Cintra. [III. A Quarrel of Authors.][4]

---

[4] Appendix III added in 1842 or soon after.

CHAPTER I

> Her thirty years of winter past,
> The red rose is reviv'd at last:
> She lifts her head for endless spring,
> For everlasting blossoming.
>
> ['Song at the Feast of Brougham Castle',
> ll. 7-10, II, 254]

So sang the Poet of the restoration of the Shepherd Lord Clifford, and he has lived to find the words apply to his own poetry. Neglected by his early contemporaries, and ridiculed by later reviewers, he has been permitted (a lot which falls to few great poets) to see their posterity do him tardy, but I trust lasting, justice. He has lived (as Mr Serjeant Talfourd has eloquently said) to see the dawn of his fame brighten the evening of his life.[5] May its sun not set till that fame has culminated!

William Wordsworth was born at Cockermouth in Cumberland, on the 7th day of April, 1770, and was the second of four sons, and older than a daughter. His father, who was of a Yorkshire family, was law-agent to the late Earl of Lonsdale, and died while the poet was young. Mr Coleridge somewhere says, that the name was originally Wadsworth, but the poet is not of that opinion. He possesses a curious carved armoury which came to him from Yorkshire, with a Latin inscription in Gothic letters, recording the making of it by William Wordsworth in the year 1525, and there is in a church in the north[6] a brass effigies of about the same date, inscribed to a Vicar of the same name, and probably the same person. Both these names are plainly spelled 'Wordesworth', which was probably the name of a place in Yorkshire.[W7]

His mother, whose maiden name was Cookson, of the Newcastle upon Tyne family, died while he was yet younger, 'lost', as he says,

> —too early for the frequent tear;

but he remembers her attending him to be catechized in church:

> How flutter'd then thy anxious heart for me,
> Beloved mother! thou whose happy hand
> Had bound the flow'rs I wore, with faithful tye;

---

[5] 'Wordsworth, now in the evening of his life, and in the dawn of his fame . . .'—Talfourd's speech on moving the second reading of the bill to amend copyright law on 25 April 1838; printed by Moxon, London 1838, p. 10. The reference dates Field's writing of the opening of Chapter I.

[6] Field first wrote, 'in the church of Dereham in Norfolk'.

[7] ?? [WW].

Sweet flow'rs, at whose inaudible command,
Her countenance, phantom-like, doth re-appear.

[*Eccl. Sonnets*, III, xxii, ll. 13, 8-12, III, 395]

After her death he was, at the age of eight years, sent to Hawkeshead School, one of the best public foundations in the north of England, endowed, in the reign of Queen Elizabeth, by Dr Edwin Sandys, Archbishop of York, the father of the translator of Ovid. Here he was educated, as were his three brothers, Dr Christopher Wordsworth, the late Dean of Bocking, and Master of Trinity College, Cambridge, being the youngest. To him the River Duddon is inscribed in some beautiful stanzas of early reminiscence. The boys were boarded in the cottage of the Dame, to whom he has alluded in the poem entitled 'Nutting'.

The poet's father died, as we have said, prematurely, and left his noble client Lord Lonsdale greatly in his debt. During his lordship's life-time, little hopes were entertained of the solution of these long unsettled accounts, between the principal and the orphan children of the deceased agent; but the present Lord Lonsdale, greatly to his honour, immediately on his cousin's death, caused an investigation by arbitrators to be made into the solicitor's claims, and a liquidation of them to be effected; and thus the family received the means of education and establishment in the world.[8] The noble earl ever since acted as the patron of the poet and his children.

[8] The following extract from the Report of the Comm^rs of Inquiry into Bankruptcy and Insolvency in 1840 evidently instances this case:

The oppression of which a tyrannical rich man may be guilty, with impunity, under the present state of the law, is well exemplified by the following facts, related by Mr Montagu, Q.C. (p. 150).

The first Lord L— was indebted to his steward about £10,000. The steward died, and his children applied for payment. The peer's reply was, "I will not pay a farthing; do your worst."—"He was, I understand, says Mr Montagu, much accustomed to consider his will as law." After various remonstrances, the children brought an action. When the case came on for trial, at Carlisle, Lo! his lordship had *retained every counsel on the circuit*, and came down with a cloud of five more witnesses! The judge ordered the case to stand over. Lord L— survived this for many years, but seems to have had no "compunctuous visitings", for he never paid one sixpence of the debt, which the sequel proved to be justly due. After his death, his successor, the present earl, most generously, most nobly, and immediately, paid all that had been claimed, with interest and costs, the whole then amounting to £25,000! "Now," says Mr Montagu, "I beg to know why that noble lord ought not to have been amenable to a process which would have compelled him either to admit or deny the debt; and, if admitted, that his property should be immediately liable for the debt; if denied, that the court should have liberty to examine as to the truth of the denial?" [BF]. The printed extract from the *Report* has been stuck onto the

Having profited largely by his studies at Hawkeshead, Mr Wordsworth in 1787 was matriculated of St John's College, Cambridge,
where he remained a sufficient length of time to obtain his bachelor's
degree in arts, without aspiring to higher academical honours. While
yet a student, he made a pedestrian excursion through part of France,
Savoy, Switzerland, and Italy, accompanied by the Revd Robert
Jones, the college-friend to whom he afterwards dedicated the poem
describing this Tour, which he published in 1793, together with the
Epistle in verse to a Young Lady (his sister) from the English Lakes.
The poet had another early friend, whose name ought not to be
omitted in any memoir of him, however slight, namely, the subject
of the following Sonnet . . .^W9

Conservative as Mr Wordsworth is, in his political opinions, there
can be no doubt that the poetical reform, for which we are indebted
to him and his friends, Mr Coleridge and Mr Southey, was greatly
influenced by the French Revolution, which was the leading event of
their youth. Their minds were thus impressed, at the most impressible
time, with the worth and rights of the many, as not made for the use
of one, or of the few. Mr Wordsworth's poetry is essentially demo-
cratic, qualify^W10 it as he may by some few political pieces: his best
sonnets are dedicated to Liberty: his most touching strains ennoble
humble life: and he will always be quoted as the poet of freedom and
of the poor:—

---

ms. The date 1840 shows that it was added for B. See Mary Moorman,
William Wordsworth, The Early Years, Oxford 1957, pp. 167-9, 558-61, on the
case, and pp. 260-1 and 265-6 on Wordsworth's friendship with Montagu
(whom Field also would almost certainly have known). The *Report*, which may
be inaccurate, gives estimates different from Moorman's of the sums involved
in settlement.

9 Field here quotes 'To the Memory of Raisley Calvert', III, 20. Line 7 was first
written as 'Where'er I lik'd, and finally array'. In a note he suggests 'Better—
Where'er I listed, and at length array'. The line has been altered in pencil to
'At my own will . . .', and to his note Field added 'Altered as in pencil by
the poet'. Variant not in de Selincourt.

10 **I am a lover of liberty, but know that liberty cannot exist apart from
order & the opinions in favor of aristocracy found in my works the
latter ones especially all arise out of the consciousness [that *del.*] I have,
that in the present state of human knowledge, & its probable state for
some ages—order cannot & therefore liberty cannot be maintained
without degrees. It [its *del.*] is pride & presumption & not a real love of
liberty which has made the french & the Americans so enamoured
of what they call equality [WW].** In B Field ignores this note although
Wordsworth thought the treatment of his political development unacceptable.
Cf. remarks about democracy in the 1835 Postscript to the 1815 Preface,
II, 444-62.

—he did love
The liberty of Man.

['Rob Roy's Grave', ll. 103-4, III, 82]

It has been said of old time, 'Once a jacobin, always a jacobin'. Mr
Coleridge asks, 'Oh, why?' But the truth is, as Mr Hazlitt states it of
Mr Southey,—'Once a philanthropist and always a philanthropist'.[11]

A considerable time before, and at the commencement of the French
Revolution, he was in Paris, where he is said to have become acquainted
with many of the leaders of the revolutionary party, and to have lived
in the same house with Brissot; and to have been driven from the
capital by the horrors of the reign of Robespierre.[W12] He himself says,
in a late [1833] poem, that he saw:

> on the soil of France,
> Rash Polity begin her maniac dance,
> Foundations broken up, the deeps run wild,
> Nor griev'd to see (himself not unbeguil'd);
> Woke from the dream, the dreamer to upbraid,
> And learn how sanguine expectations fade,
> When novel trusts by Folly are betray'd.   etc.

['The Warning', ll. 63-9, IV, 111]

Mr Hazlitt, a reformer[W13] to the last, made his first acquaintance
with Mr Wordsworth and his manuscripts, in the opening of the year
1798; and the history of that acquaintance is thus told by him in the
Liberal, vol. ii, p. 37, &c.[14]

'In the afternoon, Coleridge took me over to Allfoxden ⟨in
Somersetshire⟩ a romantic old family mansion of the St Aubins,
where Wordsworth lived. It was then in the possession of a friend of
the poet's, who gave him the free use of it. Wordsworth himself was

[11] Spirit of the Age, p. 378 [BF]. (*Complete Works*, ed. P. P. Howe, 21 vols.,
London 1930-34, Vol. XI, p. 83.)
[12] **There is much mistake here which I should like to correct in person**
[WW]. Wordsworth wrote **'a mistake'** over the clause about Brissot which,
with the next sentence, is crossed through. Mark L. Reed, *Wordsworth: The
Chronology of the Early Years*, Harvard 1967, p. 137, suggests that Field may
have borrowed from the anonymous memoir prefacing the 1828 Galignani
edition; the wording is close enough to make this virtually certain.
[13] **This implies that I was not a Reformer to the last—only my views of
reform differ greatly from Mr. Hazlitt's &c. &c.** [WW].
[14] Field quotes lengthily from 'My First Acquaintance with Poets', down to
'some spot where the continuity of his verse met with no collateral interruption'
(*Complete Works*, Vol. XVII, pp. 116-19). Only those parts of the essay which
attracted notes are given here.

from home; but his sister kept house,[W15] and set before us a frugal repast, and we had free access to her brother's poems, which were still in manuscript. . . . The next day, Wordsworth arrived from Bristol at Coleridge's cottage. I think I see him now . . . an intense, high, narrow[W16] forehead, a Roman nose, cheeks furrowed by strong purpose and feeling, and a convulsive inclination to laughter about the mouth, a good deal at variance with the solemn stately expression of the rest of his face. Chantry's bust wants the marking traits; but he was teazed into making it regular and heavy[17]. . . . Wordsworth, looking out of the low latticed window, said—"How beautifully the sun sets on that yellow bank!" I thought within myself, with what eyes these poets see nature, and, ever after, when I saw the sunset streaming upon the objects facing it, conceived I had made a discovery, or thanked Mr Wordsworth for making one for me[W18]. . .' So much from Mr Hazlitt at present.

Mr Coleridge, in his *Biographia Literaria*, has himself given a more precise account of the origin of the Lyrical Ballads:— 'During the first year that Mr Wordsworth and I were neighbours, our conversation

[5] **A mistake—I rented the house— & had no personal knowledge of the Trustees of its owner then a Minor** [WW]. 'In the. . . . house' crossed through by Wordsworth.

[6] **narrow forehead! I went thro 3 large magazines of hats in Paris, before I could find one large enough, & yet my scull is almost cut away behind** [WW]. Wordsworth crossed through 'narrow' and substituted **'broad'** in the ms. Cf. Field's 'the poet's head is . . . large and manly' in Ch. II.

[7] Coleridge said of it, that it was more like Wordsworth than Wordsworth himself was. By this he meant that it is too much idealised—that it expresses the soul of the poet and not the countenance of the man. If so, Mr Wordsworth agrees with him, and both he and Mrs Wordsworth are satisfied that it is the best likeness extant—the happiest attitude of the face, such as Sir Thomas Lawrence used to atchieve on the canvas. Mr Wordsworth informed me that he prepared Sir Francis Chantry's mind for it, by repeating to him those stanzas of the 'Poet's Epitaph', beginning

But who is he with modest looks, etc. [l. 37 ff., IV, 66]

Mr W. considers Mr Pickersgill's portraits of him earthy and lumpish, compared with the great sculptor's 'animated bust' [BF].

Here Field has an interesting but awkwardly long note, on which Wordsworth comments. It begins with a passage from De Quincey in *Tait's Magazine* [1839; but not in De Quincey's revised version of the objectionable articles of that year in *Works*, ed. Masson, 14 vols, Edinburgh 1890, Vol. II, pp. 229-332] to the effect that Wordsworth's deficient sensibility to music was balanced by an unusual sensibility to certain modes of visual beauty. Although his judgment of painting was unsound, he and Dorothy derived from the forms and colouring of rural nature a pleasure 'originally and organically more profound than is often witnessed'. Field then aptly quotes:

The Memoirs

turned frequently on the two cardinal points of poetry . . .'[19] And so
much at present from Mr Coleridge.

The next record we find of Mr Wordsworth's poetical history is in
Mr Joseph Cottle's Early Recollections of Coleridge, vol. i p. 298,
&c . . .[20] 'A reference was made by Mr Coleridge, in one of these
letters, to the "caballing long and loud" against Mr Wordsworth, and

---

> Such delight I found
> To note in shrub and tree, in stone and flower,
> That intermixture of delicious hues,
> Along so vast a surface, all at once,
> In one impression, by connecting force
> Of their own beauty, imag'd in the heart.
> ['To Joanna', ll. 45-50, II, 113]

He then writes, 'This is the only extract I shall make from the papers of this
writer. He avows a quarrel with Mr Wordsworth; and his portraits of the poet
his wife and sister, are consequently not only unfavorable likenesses, but
unwarrantable exposures, especially as published during their lifetime. Mr
Hazlitt's only objections to Mr Wordsworth are critical and political; and there
is, in his portrait of the poet, in the next chapter, nothing inconsistent with
not only admiration of the author, which Mr De Quincey still retains, but
with love of the man, which that writer disclaims'. Against 'unwarrantable
exposures . . .' Wordsworth has his own long and angry note: **Not so
much as published during their lives as published or intended to be
published at all. The man has written under the influence of wounded
feelings as he avows, I am told; for I have never read a word of his
infamous production, nor ever shall. My acquaintance with him was
the result of a letter of his own volunteered to me. He was 7 months
an inmate of my house; and by what breach of the laws of hospitality
that kindness was repaid, his performance, if rightly represented to me
sufficiently shows. A man who can set such an example, I hold to be
pest in society, and one of the most worthless of mankind. They who
know me best could testify, did they think it worth while to notice the
thing, that my fault was only that of bearing with him his character
and proceedings far more tenderly than I ought to have done. The
particulars shall never by me be recorded.** See M. Moorman, William
Wordsworth, The Later Years, Oxford 1965, pp. 234-37, for an account of the
incident to which Wordsworth presumably refers. In B Field omits the first
sentence of Wordsworth's note.

[19] Field quotes from 'Biog. Lit. vol. ii, p1 &c' (Biographia Literaria, ed. J. Shawcross
2 vols, Oxford 1907, Vol. II, pp. 5-8), down to 'the author's own practice
the greater number of the poems themselves', without comment except for
note of Coleridge's contributions to Lyrical Ballads.

[20] Field here reproduces several pages from Cottle, Early Recollections . . ., 2 vol
London 1837 (repr. 1970), Vol. I, p. 298-Vol. II, p. 27, passim. His extract
include the following letters: Early Letters . . ., ed. E. de Selincourt, Oxfo
1935, rev. ed. Chester L. Shaver, 1967, pp. 215, 219 ('We look for you . .
without ps.), 259, 261-2 (see n. 1 p. 262), 269; Letters of Samuel Taylor Coleridge
ed. E. L. Griggs, 6 vols, Oxford 1956-71, Vol. I, pp. 399, 402, 411-13. In o

28

which occasioned him to remove from Somersetshire.W21 To learn the nature of this annoyance may furnish some little amusement to the reader, while Mr Wordsworth himself will only smile at trifling incidents, that are now perhaps scarcely remembered . . .' [Cottle here gives the supposed village tales that Wordsworth was a night-wanderer, a mutterer in outlandish brogue, a conjuror, a smuggler, a secret distiller, a French jacobin ('for he is so silent and dark, that nobody ever heard him say one word about politics').]

The volume of the Lyrical Ballads ⟨continues Mr Cottle⟩ was published about Midsummer 1798. In September of the same year, Mr Coleridge and Mr Wordsworth left England for Germany,[22] and I for ever quitted the business of a bookseller. . . . I have been the more particular in these statements, as they furnish perhaps the most remarkable instance on record of a volume of poems remaining for so long a time almost totally neglected, and afterwards acquiring, and that almost as rapidly, so much deserved popularity.' And so much for Mr Cottle.

Mr Wordsworth told the writer of these pages in 1828, that he had never derived any pecuniary advantage from his subsequent poems, with the exception of fifty guineas, which he received for a few

---

note Field points out that although it was easy to mock Cottle, as Byron had done, 'When we consider how maiden poets are generally treated by booksellers, and their "virgin muse" by periodical critics, this narrative [of the acceptance of *Lyrical Ballads*, 1798] is highly creditable to the writer's sagacity, as well as to his generosity'. Another note quotes *Biog. Lit.* I, 58-9. There is footnote discussion of the reception of *Lyrical Ballads* and a separate note of Appendix I, into which most of this discussion was taken. Some footnote remarks about the relation between *Salisbury Plain* and 'The Female Vagrant' are corrected, in preparation for B, to record the publication of *Guilt and Sorrow* in 1842.

21 **A mistake.** *Not the occasion* **of my removal. Annoyances I had none. The facts mentioned by Coleridge of a spy, &c, came not to my knowledge till I had left the neighbourhood. I was not refused a continuance. I never applied for one** [WW]. See Moorman, *The Early Years*, pp. 328-32.

22 The only memorials of this Tour are to be found in Mr Coleridge's 'Friend' and in his Biographia Literaria. The authors of the Lyrical Ballads visited Klopstock, but not Schiller or Goethe; but they were doubtless attracted to that country by sympathy with that poetical reform, which was begun by Bürger and Lessing, and after this time was perfected by Goëthe in Germany; and which was begun in England by Dr Percy and perfected by Mr Wordsworth [BF]. Wieland's name is crossed out and replaced by those of Bürger and Lessing, perhaps after Wordsworth's reading of the ms. Field would not have known of Dorothy Wordsworth's record of the tour (*Journals*, ed. E. de Selincourt, 2 vols, Oxford 1941, Vol. I, pp. 17-34).

contributions to the Keepsake for 1829.[23] I know what Mr Cottle calls popularity. I should think he means notoriety. The Lyrical Ballads were republished in Mr Wordsworth's name, with a second volume of other poems and the celebrated Preface, in 1800, after which they were [with the exception of two or three small editions] never reprinted[W24] till, combined with his two more duodecimo volumes of Poems of 1807, in the year 1815, in two octavo volumes; and that not till after the year 1814 had called the attention of the public to his name by the important publication of the Excursion; and in 1815 was also published the White Doe of Rylstone. Both these last were printed in quarto, as was then the expensive fashion. To conclude the list of Mr Wordsworth's works,—in the year 1816 was published the Thanksgiving Ode on the Peace, in 1819 Peter Bell and the Waggoner; in 1820 the River Duddon and other poems, with a prose description of the Lakes in the north of England; in 1822 the Ecclesiastical Sonnets; and lastly in 1835 Yarrow Revisited and many other poems. In 1820

[23] Actually 100 guineas, paid early in 1828 for contributions for the *Keepsake* for Christmas 1828. See Moorman, *Later Years*, p. 453. This may indicate a missing 1828 letter from Wordsworth to Field.

[24] I rather think there are mistakes here.

First Ed published in 1 vol	1798
Second with a 2d vol	1800
Third Ed the date forgotten	[1802]
Fourth Ed (now before me)	1805
Fifth Ed - - - -	1815
Sixth Ed - - - -	1820
Seventh 5 vols - - -	1827
Eighth 4 vols - - -	1832
Ninth } 6 vols	1837 } Stereotype
Tenth }	1839 }

I am inclined to think there was also an Ed between the fourth & fifth [*Poems in Two Volumes*?], as here marked, but I cannot make it out—there have been also to my knowledge 5 American editions—copies of 3 of which I possess—Gagliani's [*sic*, for Galignani] foreman owned to me that their Ed. printed in 1828 amounted to 3000 copies—I was told by others much more—this Ed. I know interfered greatly among my own countrymen with the English sale. Notwithstanding the above statement the pecuniary profit to me which was the only thing I cared much about (tho' I never *wrote a line for money* [merely *inserted and del.*] in my life & not a word except the few contributions to the Keepsake, with the least view towards it), was [small *del.*] trifling—owing to the heavy bills brought against me in the usual way of the Trade by the Publisher — & the smallness of the Eds exceeding in no case till within the last 10 years 1000 copies [WW]. Wordsworth began to write on Field's page, then started again on a separate sheet which Field stuck into his ms. In B Field refers misleadingly to 'a letter with which he favoured me in the year 1840, when the subject of the remuneration of authors was before the legislature and the public'.

the whole of the poet's verses then published, except the Excursion were collected in four volumes 12mo. In 1821 the Excursion was reprinted in 8vo; in 1827 the whole, including the Excursion, were published in five volumes; and in 1833, they were compressed into four pocket volumes. All the foregoing publications issued from the house of Messieurs Longman and company. In 1836-7 the whole of Mr Wordsworth's poetical works, in six small 8vo volumes were classed and stereotyped for immortality by Mr Moxon the publisher, who paid the author a thousand guineas for the copyright of the stereotype, from which five thousand copies have already been struck off; and in 1838, the Sonnets were collected into one volume with a few additional ones. This makes not more than six[W25] reprints in forty years.

The poems of 1815 were dedicated to Sir George Beaumont; the Excursion in a perfect sonnet to Lord Lonsdale, Peter Bell to Mr Southey, the Waggoner to Mr Lamb, Yarrow Revisited to Mr Rogers, [and Memorials of his last Tour to Mr Crabb Robinson].[26] These are or were his friends.

Mr Wordsworth is also the author of two pamphlets, the first in 1809 entitled '. . . the Convention of Cintra . . .'. Of this pamphlet, Mr Coleridge, in the 'Friend', said— 'If my readers wish to see the question of the efficacy of principles and popular opinions, for evil and for good, proved and illustrated with an eloquence worthy of the subject, I can refer them, with the hardiest anticipation of their thanks, to the late work by my honoured friend William Wordsworth, quem quoties lego, non verba mihi videor audire, sed tonitrua'. Soon after its publication however, this pamphlet was suppressed partly out of deference to the opinions of the poet's friend Lord Lonsdale, and partly out of delicacy to Sir Arthur Wellesley (as he then was), who was considered even then to have atoned for his subordinate share in the disgrace of this convention, by the previous victory of Vimiero, and who soon afterwards effaced all memory of it by that of Talavera.

This pamphlet being now exceedingly scarce, I deem it right in the Appendix [II] to this little work, to rescue from suppression the eloquent summing up of it, which shows that had Mr Wordsworth continued his political studies, he would have followed the steps of Milton in his prose as well as in his poetical writings; and also another passage which proves that Mr Wordsworth's thoughts on public

---

[25] **A mistake I am persuaded** [WW]. Field later crossed through the sentence and substituted 'In 1842 was published the volume of Poems chiefly of early and late years, forming the 7th volume'.

[26] The *Memorials* (III, 202-29) of the Italian tour of 1837, with the dedication, was published in 1842.

liberty and private judgment continue to be as philosophical and independent as the poetry of his earlier years.

After this time the campaign in the Peninsula proceeded more prosperously and Mr Wordsworth was justified in exchanging his thunders of war for a music of peace. Early in 1816 he published his Thanksgiving Ode and a few other Poems as a sequel to his Sonnets to Liberty; and his next prose pamphlet, not political but literary, appeared in the same year in the shape of 'A Letter to a friend of Robert Burns . . .' This pamphlet contained a vindication of Burns from an article in the Edinburgh Review. Mr Wordsworth also contributed the masterly Essay on Epitaphs, and the reply to Mr Wilson's letter, which appear in the 'Friend'.

CHAPTER II The contemplative and retired life, which Mr Wordsworth always passed, admits of few other records than the dates of his successive publications, for his poetry itself traces his travels in those

> memorial rhymes
> That animate my way where'er it leads.

['On Revisiting Dunnolly Castle', ll. 13-14, IV, 37]

In the year 1800, we find the poet settled at Grasmere in Westmoreland, from whence he removed to his present residence at Rydal Mount in the same neighbourhood. In 1803, he married his cousin Miss Mary Hutchinson, the daughter of a merchant at Penrith, by whom he had several children, of whom two sons and a daughter survive.[27] To his wife, the White Doe of Rylstone is inscribed in some exquisite stanzas, and latterly the Miscellaneous Sonnets, in a new opening one, besides the concluding. He was driven by the unprofitableness of his poems, to eke out his little patrimony by the acceptance in the year 1813 of the office of Distributor of Stamps for the district of Whitehaven,[W28] an appointment which he owed to the constant friendship of the Earl of Lonsdale.

In his early Scottish travels, the poet's sister was his companion, as may be seen by her interesting journals, which are quoted in the Life of Sir Walter Scott [1837-8], as well as in Mr Wordsworth's volumes.

In the autumn of 1820, Mr Wordsworth with his wife[W29] and their

[27] Several words have been obliterated here.
[28] **Westmoreland & ½ of Cumberland** [WW]. Whitehaven is crossed out.
[29] **sister.** WW's insertion after 'wife'.

friend Mr Henry Crabb Robinson, made a long tour in Switzerland as far as the north of Italy, the fruits of which ripened into those 'Memorials of a Tour on the Continent', which form some of the most delightful of the author's poems, and are inscribed in a sonnet to those 'dear fellow-travellers'.

In 1828, thirty years after their first visit to Germany, Mr Wordsworth and Mr Coleridge were permitted to enjoy the pleasure of revisiting the Rhine, as far as Bergen [*sic* A and B, for Bingen]. And lastly in 1837, Mr Wordsworth, again with Mr Robinson, 'paid the magnificent debt, due to the beauty of Florence, the grandeur of Rome' [cf. 'Stanzas Composed in the Simplon Pass', ll. 9 and 12, III, 189].

I take the opportunity of publishing an extract from Mr Robinson's letter to me on this occasion:—

'We set out on the 19th March. Of our journey take this rapid sketch. We bore with patience the fatigue of posting through France, and were recompensed by three glorious days between Nice and Genoa, and between Genoa and Spezia. I will name, as valuable intimations, what Wordsworth enjoyed most on the journey. He felt much more the beauties of nature, than the wonders of art. Even Pisa did not excite him (or Nismes before) as much as I expected. He cared little for the Etruscan city of Volterra or Sienna. During our month's stay at Rome, he seemed deeply impressed above all by St Peter's. His eye for colour seems more cultivated than his sense of form: at least the picture-galleries were more attractive to him than the museums of sculpture. But in general, he will not allow the plastic artist of any kind to place himself by the side of the poet, as his equal. And in this he is beyond all doubt right. He felt the pathetic grandeur of the environs of Rome, and regretted that bad weather did not allow him to visit all the spots of the adjacent mountains, in romantic interest the most profoundly attractive of any place that has a name upon the earth. But I showed him the Nemi and Albano, and the Monte Cavo and Tivoli, after taking him to the top of the Colosseum, and round the arches of triumph, and the columns, and the aqueducts, and the walls of Rome. The dread of the quarantine,[30] so strictly enforced by the Roman government, deterred us from going to Naples. We returned by Florence, taking care, after seeing Terni, to digress from the high road, and visit the three monasteries of L'Averna, Camaldoli and Vallombrosa. I mention this that you may do the same one day. At L'Averna he heard the cuckoo. It was an awakening incident to him, and one day the world will know that the cuckoo may be heard amid the

[30] It was then the time of the *cholera morbus* [BF, in B].

haunts of San Francesco d'Assisi.[31] We pursued our course through Modena and Parma to Milan; whence we went again on the lake of Como; and afterwards made excursions (to Wordsworth's great joy) on the lakes of Iseo and La Guarda. We saw Brescia, Verona, Vicenza, Padua, and above all Venice. We then passed over a newly-formed road to the west of the Tyrol, in Styria, to Salzburg, a place of marvellous attractions; devoted a week to the Austrian Salzkammer Gut (Salt Domain); and having seen the most famous of the Bavarian lakes and the fine works of art at Munich, and paused a little at Heidelberg and Brussells, reached London on the 7th August.'[32]

While the poet was abroad on this occasion, Mr Serjeant Talfourd pronounced on him the following noble eulogy, from his place in the House of Commons, on moving for leave to bring in a bill to extend the term of authors' copyright . . .[33]

This bill is still in suspense. Let us hope that it will become the law of the land, long before Mr Wordsworth's earlier copyrights expire with him. We are now anxiously expecting some fruits of the poet's last tour—a few effusions like the 'Pillar of Trajan' [III, 229-31]—even if it should not be permitted to us to receive any further portion of the 'Recluse'.

In the year 1838, the new University of Durham did itself the honour of conferring its first honorary degree of LL.D.[34] upon our

---

[31] Among the poems of the late Professor Carlyle, 4to, 1805, there are some elegant stanzas on hearing a cuckoo in the valley of St Saba in Asia Minor. [Added for B: In 1842, W. Wordsworth's 7th volume included his Memorials of this Tour in Italy, inscribed to Mr. Robinson.] [BF]. The poem referred to is 'The Cuckoo at Laverna', III, 218. See Field's letter of 16 November 1837, quoted in introduction.

[32] This interesting letter is not in *The Correspondence of Crabb Robinson with the Wordsworth Circle*, ed. E. J. Morley, 2 vols, Oxford 1927.

[33] Field here quotes from Talfourd's speech on 18 May 1837: 'The term allowed by the existing law is curiously adapted to encourage the lightest works, and to leave the noblest unprotected. . . . I refer to one, who "in this setting-part of Time", has opened a vein of the deepest sentiment and thought before unknown—who has supplied the noblest antidote to the freezing effects of the scientific spirit of the age—who, while he has detected that poetry, which is the essence of the greatest things, has cast a glory around the lowest conditions of humanity, and traced out the subtle links, by which they are connected with the highest. . . . Shall the law, whose term has been amply sufficient to his scorners, now afford him no protection, because he has outlasted their scoffs, because his flame has been fostered amidst the storms, and is now the growth of years?'. Printed Moxon, London 1837, pp. 12-14. Field added for B the sentence, 'It was not till the year 1842 when Sir Robert Peel returned to the helm of government that a bill was carried for the extension of authors' copyright', and deleted the following paragraph.

[34] Actually DCL. See Moorman, *Later Years*, p. 452.

poet; and in the following year, he was invested with the same honorary distinction by the convocation of Oxford.

[Dr Arnold writes:— 'I went up to Oxford to the Commemoration for the first time for twenty-one years, to see Wordsworth and Bunsen receive their degrees; and to me, remembering how old Coleridge inoculated a little knot of us with the love of Wordsworth, when his name was in general a by-word, it was striking to witness the thunders of applause, repeated over and over again, with which he was greeted in the theatre, by the undergraduates and masters of arts alike'.[35]]

His portrait had previously been painted by Mr Pickersgill for his own college of St John's, Cambridge, and again for Sir Robert Peel—his bust has been finely sculptured by Sir Francis Chantry—and his effigy has been appropriately introduced by Mr Haydon into his great picture of Christ's Entry into Jerusalem, as the contrast of Voltaire. From these works of art, it will be seen that the poet's head is, like his mind, large and manly, and not petty and childish, as he has been misrepresented. His voice is peculiarly deep and melodious, and his countenance solemn and meditative. He thinks more than he reads, and employs a great part of his time in walking about his own lakes and mountains. He is not one of those, of whom Coleridge says:—

Poet, who hath been building up the rhyme . . .[36]

Mr Wordsworth is, as he says of himself,

A poet, one who loved the brooks
Far better than the sages' books.

['The Idle Shepherd Boys', ll. 84-5, I, 238] . . .[37]

---

[35] Stanley's Life of Arnold, vol. ii, p. 160 [BF]. Stanley's *Life* was published in May 1844, thus dating this B paragraph.
[36] 'The Nightingale', ll. 24-34 and 40-41, *Poems*, ed. E. H. Coleridge, 2 vols, Oxford 1912, Vol. I, p. 264.
[37] On the facing pp. Field has inserted sts 3-8 of 'The Tables Turned', IV, 57, and further material for B. This includes the remarks, 'If I were asked what was the leading characteristic of Mr Wordsworth's mind, I should say strong-manly sense, which, to be sure, is the *principium et fons* of all arts and sciences. . . . He was a man of business, as well as a poet. His official letters to the Commissioners of Stamps would prove this. He used to take the lead in travelling parties. He once related to me an interesting anecdote of his perseverance in punishing a *voiturier* in Switzerland, who had detained his cloak for nonpayment of an overcharge. Poetical justice was completely obtained at last, but the persons were very troublesome and prosaic. The poet's father was a man of law, and if he had lived, Mr Wordsworth would, in all probability, have been a barrister. He had, in conversation, all the ready acuteness of a legal practitioner. He was very eloquent, in favour of the Copyright bill, and said to me that he should like to walk into the House of Commons, and speak upon it *extempore*;

The following portrait, with all its exaggerations, is too excellent to be omitted in any memoir of the Poet. It appeared in 1825, in Mr Hazlitt's 'Spirit of the Age' . . .[38] 'It is fine to hear him talk of the way, in which certain subjects have been treated by eminent poets, according to his notions of the art. Thus he finds fault with Dryden's description of Bacchus in the Alexander's Feast, as if he were a mere good-looking youth, or boon companion—

> Flush'd with a purple grace,
> He shows his honest face—

instead of representing the god, returning from the conquest of India, crowned with vine leaves, and followed by troops of satyrs, of wild men and animals that he had tamed.[39] You would think, on hearing him speak on this subject, that you saw Titian's picture of the meeting of Bacchus and Ariadne, so classic were his conceptions, so glowing his style. Milton is his great idol, and he sometimes dares to compare himself with him. His sonnets, indeed, have something of the same high-raised tone and prophetic spirit. Chaucer is another prime favorite of his; and he has been at the pains to modernize some of the Canterbury Tales. Those persons, who look upon Mr Wordsworth as a merely puerile writer, must be rather at a loss to account for his strong predilection for such geniuses as Dante and Michael Angelo. We do not think our author has any cordial sympathy with Shakspeare.[W40] How should he? Shakspeare was the least of an egotist of any body in the world. He does not much relish the variety and scope of dramatic composition. "He hates those interlocutions between Lucius and

---

and there is no doubt he could have done it. ... He had chosen the contemplative life as best adapted to his vocation, but he would have shone in the active world, and would probably have acquired riches in it.'

[38] *Complete Works*, Vol. XI, pp. 91-5. Only passages attracting notes of interest are given.

[39] Since Mr Hazlitt wrote, Mr Wordsworth has exhibited the following comment in his '[On the] Power of Sound': [ll. 147-52, II, 328]. ... This 'Power of Sound' is a very noble and philosophical poem; but Mr Wordsworth would be more at home in the 'Power of Colour'. He has often been told that he had spoiled a good lawyer; but what a painter he would have made! Multifariousness is the characteristic of all men of genius [BF]. Cf. n. 18, and Field's comment in letter of 17 December 1836, quoted in introduction.

[40] **This is monstrous! I extol Chaucer & others because the world at large knows little or nothing of their merits. Modesty & deep feeling how superfluous a thing it is to praise Shakespere have kept me often & almost habitually silent upon that subject. Who thinks it necessary to praise the Sun? [WW]**

Caius.''[41] Yet Mr Wordsworth himself wrote a tragedy when he was young; and we have heard the following energetic lines quoted from it, as put into the mouth of a person, smit with remorse for some rash crime:—

> Action is momentary—a step, a blow,
> The motion of a muscle—this way or that—
> 'Tis done; and in the after-vacancy
> We wonder at ourselves, like men betray'd;
> Suffering is permanent, obscure and dark,
> And has the nature of infinity.[42]
>
> [*The Borderers*, ll. 1539-44, I, 188]

Perhaps for want of light and shade, and the unshackled spirit of the drama, this performance was never brought forward.

'Our poet has a great dislike to Gray, and a fondness for Thomson and Collins. It is mortifying to hear him speak of Pope and Dryden,[W43] whom, because they have been supposed to have all the possible excellencies of poetry, he will allow to have none. Nothing however can be fairer than the way, in which he sometimes exposes the un-

---

[41] Mr Wordsworth's genius certainly is not dramatic; but such passages of his poetry, as have already passed into classical quotations read more like Shakspeare than like any other author. Had he no sympathy with

> that darling Bard,
> Who told of Juliet and her Romeo,
> And of the lark's note heard before its time,
> And of the streaks that lac'd the severing clouds
> In the unrelenting East?
>
> ['Vaudracour and Julia', ll. 90-94, II, 62]   [BF]

[42] Field thus corrects in a note Hazlitt's misquotation. Wordsworth said in 1837 that the lines 'were either read or recited by me more than thirty years since, to the late Mr Hazlitt, who quoted some expressions in them (imperfectly remembered) in a work of his published some years ago' (III, 548-9). See n. 48.

[43] **Monstrous again—I have ten times the knowledge of Pope's writings & of Dryden's also, that ever this writer had—to this day I believe I could repeat with a little previous rummaging of my memory several 1000 lines of Pope—But if the beautiful the pathetic & the sublime be what a Poet should chiefly aim at how absurd is it to place these men among the first Poets of their Country—admirable are they in treading their way but that way lies almost at the foot of Parnassus** [WW]. Wordsworth has underlined 'It is mortifying ... Dryden' and 'he will allow to have none'. Field later added, 'Mr Wordsworth's genius has a kindredness with that of Pope's poetry, though an antipathy to that of his style. The human heart and character is the great province of both poets, and not mere descriptive landskip—nor "arms and the man"—nor "the dragon's wing, the magic ring"'.

meaning verbiage of modern poetry. Thus in the beginning of Dr Johnson's Vanity of Human Wishes,

> Let Observation, with extensive view,
> Survey mankind, from China to Peru,

he says there is a total want of imagination accompanying the words—the same idea is repeated three times, under the disguise of a different phraseology—it comes to this—Let Observation, with extensive observation, observe mankind. Take away the first line, and the second—

> Survey mankind from China to Peru,

literally conveys the whole.[44] Mr Wordsworth is, we must say, a perfect Drawcansir as to prose-writers. . . . He approves of Walton's Angler, Paley and some other writers of an inoffensive modesty of pretension[45] . . . in pronouncing Rembrandt to be a man of genius, he feels that he strengthens his own claim to the title[46]. . . . He has gnawed too much on the bridle, and has often thrown out crusts to the critics

---

[44] Here Field has a perceptive but wordy note in Johnson's defence. He quotes Johnson's comment to Boswell on the adjective in 'illustrious Iona' (that it contributes nothing as to fact but wakes the mind to peculiar attention) as one parallel; suggests that the second line of 'The Vanity of Human Wishes' without the first would be 'too particular, and not inclusive of the whole globe—scarcely intelligible'; and offers instructive comparisons with Johnson's Horatian model, with Dryden's more economical rendering ('this is very prosaic, and all picturesqueness is lost by the omission of the names of any part of the world'), with passages of Pope, and with an abridgement by the Abbé Gaultier of the first ten lines of *Paradise Lost* to 'Muse of Moses, sing of Man's first disobedience' ('Paradise Lost, with all the poetry left out'). He concludes with an example of Pope's translation of Horace which he thinks 'affords a real instance of a repetition of the same idea': 'Vain was the chief's, the sage's pride: They had no poet and they died. In Vain they schem'd—in vain they bled—They had no poet, and are dead'.

[45] Was the 'divine right of constables' inoffensive? It lost its author a bishoprick, like Swift's 'Tale of a Tub' [BF].

[46] This calls to my mind a few lines, which the poet condescended to write in Mrs Field's Album, opposite to a pen and ink sketch thereon, by a relative of mine, of just such a nature as (however inferior to) an etching of Rembrandt's:— [Field here quotes 'Written in Mrs Field's Album', IV, 387]. What a fine line is 'No witchery of inky words' [BF]. Field adds a few lines of his own (see IV, 478) and two other quotations. His letter of 24 December 1828 requested the album entry and he acknowleged it in his letter of 26 February 1829. Wordsworth's note about Edmund Field's drawing and his own lines of 19 January 1829, given as a separate entry (following Knight) without an addressee in *Letters, Later Years*, I, 347, is probably in fact a postscript to the immediately preceding letter to Barron Field of the same date.

in mere defiance, as a point of honour, when he was challenged, which otherwise his own good sense would have withheld.[47] We suspect that Mr Wordsworth's feelings are a little morbid in this respect, or that he resents censure more than he is gratified with praise. Otherwise the tide has turned much in his favour of late years; he has a large body of determined partisans; and is at present sufficiently in request with the public, to save or relieve him from the last necessity to which a man of genius can be reduced,—that of becoming the god of his own idolatry.'[W48]

I shall conclude these Characters of the Poet by the following, which was published anonymously in the Edinburgh Annual Register for 1808, but which is now understood to be from the elegant pen of Sir Walter Scott:— 'Although hitherto an unsuccessful competitor for poetical fame, as far as it depends upon the general voice of the public, no man has ever considered the character of the poet as more honorable, or his pursuit as more important, than Mr Wordsworth. . . . Even so the impressions made upon the susceptible mind of the solitary poet, by common and unimportant incidents, and the train of "sweet and bitter fancies", to which they give rise, are, in the eye of the public, altogether extravagant, and disproportioned to their cause.'[49]

CHAPTER III When Mr Wordsworth first collected his whole works in 1827, he made sundry alterations in them, in deference to Mr Jeffrey's Edinburgh Review, which appeared to me to injure their simplicity; and I took the freedom of expostulating with the great

[47] I shall endeavour to show, in a subsequent Chapter [III?], that he has conceded too much to critics, at least in his practice [BF].

[48] These observations are for the first time read by me— & so may I say of the larger part of the quotations you have honored by yr notice— The [favorable accept *del.*] reception of my poems would have been quite as favorable as I could wish but for the conceited stupidity of certain leading Reviewers—for which I cared very little excepting my means of purchasing books & obtaining other intellectual gratifications which would have been within my reach had I and the public been fairly dealt with [WW]. But Wordsworth's comment given in n. 42 shows that he had read Hazlitt's essay. Cf. n. 110.

[49] Field here quotes for several pages without comment. The passage is on pp. 428-30 of 'On the Living Poets of Great Britain', *Edinburgh Annual Register for 1808*, 1810, Vol. I, Pt 2, pp. 417-43. M. Ball, *Sir Walter Scott as a Critic of Literature*, New York 1907, pp. 118 n. 3, 165, suggests from internal evidence that the essay was heavily influenced by Scott and may have been dictated or written, in part or whole, by him. Field's comment may support her attribution. The article does not 'hesitate to distinguish as the most successful candidates for poetical praise, Scott, Southey and Campbell' (p. 419).

poet upon these refinements. In answer to my letter, I was honoured
by the following explanation:—

Letter I[50]

Rydal Mount, 24th Octr [*sic*, for April] 1828.

My dear Sir,
   I will not spend time in thanking you for your kindness, but will
go at once to the point, and to the strongest case, 'The Beggars' [II,
222]. I will state the faults, real or supposed, which put me on the task
of altering it.

What other dress she had I could not know,

you must allow is a villainous line, one of the very worst in my whole
writings, I hope so at least. 'In all my walks', I thought obtrusively
personal.

Her face was of Egyptian brown.

The style, or rather composition, of this whole stanza is what I call
bricklaying, formal accumulation of particulars.

Pouring out sorrows like a sea,

I did not like; and *sea* clashes with 'was beautiful to see' below. 'On
English land' is the same rhyme as 'gayest of the land' in the stanza
below. Such were the reasons for altering. Now for the success.

Nor claimed she service from the hood,

is (I own) an expression too pompous for the occasion; and if you could
substitute a line for the villainous 'What other dress' &c. I would
willingly part with it. But there is still a difficulty.

She had a tall man's height or more;

would anticipate

---

[50] This important letter save for the concluding sentences is in *Letters, Later Years*,
I, 307–13. de Selincourt has preferred Knight's incomplete version in his
Letters of the Wordsworth Family, 3 vols, London 1907, Vol. III, pp. 412–20, to
the more accurate version in his *Life*, Vol. III, pp. 150–6, apparently taken from
B. In Knight's *Letters*, and consequently in de Selincourt, two of Field's notes
have inadvertently been absorbed into the text and Wordsworth's conclusion
omitted (see nn. 59, 62 and 64). The A version is given here in full (with Field's
obviously wrong date corrected) as probably the more accurate. The restora-
tions referred to in nn. below were made in 1836. (In Ch. IX Field gives the
texts of the 1815, 1827 and 1836 versions of 'The Beggars'.) See Appendix for
Field's letters.

> She tower'd, fit person &c.

The boys could well understand *looking* reproof. There is frowning, shaking the head, &c. 'Telling me a lie' might be restored without much objection on my part,[51] for 'Heaven hears that rash reply' is somewhat too refined; but as

> It was your mother, as I say,

is retained, the fact is implied of my knowledge of their having told an untruth. It is not to be denied that I have aimed at giving more elegance and dignity to this poem, partly on its own account, and partly that it might harmonize better with the one appended to it. I thought I had succeeded in my attempt better than, it seems, I have done. You will observe that in any meditated alteration of the first stanza, which I should be very thankful if you would do for me, the word *head* cannot be used, on account of '*head* those antient Amazonian files', in the stanza below.

The Blind Highland Boy. [III, 88]

The 'shell' was substituted for the 'washing-tub', on the suggestion of Coleridge; and greatly as I respect your opinion and Lamb's, I cannot now bring myself to undo my work, though if I had been aware beforehand that such judges would have objected, I should not have troubled myself with making the alteration. I met the other day with a pretty picture of hazardous navigation like this. I think it is on the coast of Madras, where people are described as trusting themselves to the rough waves on small rafts, in such a way that the flat surface being hidden from view by the billows, the navigator appears to be sitting on the bare waters.

Rural Architecture. [I, 244]

'From the meadows of Armath,' &c. My sister objected so strongly to this alteration at the time, that,—her judgment being confirmed by your's,—the old reading may be restored.

Pedestrian Tour among the Alps.
[*Descr. Sketches*, 1793, ll. 788-91, I, 88]

> No more, along thy vales and viny groves,
> Whole hamlets disappearing as he moves,
> With cheeks o'erspread by smiles of baleful glow,
> On his pale horse shall fell Consumption go.

[51] It is now restored [BF].

I had utterly forgotten this passage: at all events, as a bold juvenile thing, it might be restored. I suppose I must have written it, from its being applied here in my mind, not to an individual but to a people.

Ruth. [II, 227]

And there exulting in her wrongs,
Among the music of her songs,
She fearfully caroused.

This was altered, Lamb having observed that it was not English. I liked it better myself; but certainly to carouse cups, that is to empty them, is the genuine English.[52]

The Sailor's Mother. [II, 54]

And, thus continuing, she said,
I had a son, who *many a day*
Sailed on the seas.

The last words shall be restored. I suppose I had objected to the first line, which, it must be allowed, is rather flat.

He to a fellow-lodger's care
Had left it to be watch'd and fed
Till he came back again.

Than this last line,

And pipe its song in safety,

I own, strikes me as better, because 'from the bodings of his mind', he feared he should not come back again. He might dramatically have said to his fellow-lodger—'Take care of this bird till I come back again', not liking to own to another, or to himself even, in words, that he feared he should not return; but as he is not introduced here speaking, it is, I think, better; and brings in a pretty image of the bird singing, when its master might be in peril, or no more.[53]

The Emigrant Mother. [II, 56]

Smiles hast thou, bright ones of thy own;
I cannot keep thee in my arms,

[52] It now stands:

And there with many a doleful song
And of wild words, her cup of wrong
She fearfully caroused.

What a happy restoration! [BF]

[53] What a lesson in poetry is this! [BF]

> For they confound me; as it is,
> I have forgot those smiles of his.

Coleridge objected to the last two lines, for which

> By those bewildering glances crost,
> In which the light of his is lost,

is substituted. The alteration ought, in my judgment, to be retained.[54]

The Idiot Boy. [II, 67]

'Across the saddle' much better. So 'up towards', instead of 'up upon' in *Michael* [II, 80].

The Green Linnet. [II, 139]

> A brother of the leaves he seems,

may be thus retained:—

> My sight he dazzles—nay deceives:
> He seems a brother of the leaves.

The stanza, as you have been accustomed to quote it, is very faulty. 'Forth he *teems*' is a provincialism, Dr Johnson says 'a low word, when used in this sense'. But my main motive for altering this stanza was the wholly unjustifiable use of the word *train* as applied to leaves attached to a tree. A train of *withered* leaves, driven in the wind along the gravel, as I have often seen them, sparkling in April sunshine, might be said. '*Did* feign' is also an awkward expletive for an elegant poem, as this is generally allowed to be.[W55]

To the small Celandine. ['To the Same', II, 144]

'Old Magellan' shall be restored.

To the Daisy. [IV, 67]

> Thou wander'st the wide world about,
> &c. &c. &c.

I was loath to part with this stanza. It may either be restored, or printed at the end of a volume, among notes and variations, when you edite [*sic*] the fifteenth edition.[56]

---

[54] The lines now run thus:—

> For they confound me;—where, where is
> That last, that sweetest, smile of his?   [BF]

[55] 'for an . . . to be' crossed out with a wavering line in A (but retained in B), presumably by Wordsworth, who might have been embarrassed to re-read such a remark.

[56] It is now restored [BF].

To a Skylark. [II, 141]

After having succeeded so well in the second 'Skylark' [II, 266][57] and in the conclusion of the poem entitled 'A Morning Exercise' [II, 124], in my notice of this Bird, I became indifferent to this poem, which Coleridge used severely to condemn, and to treat contemptuously. I like however the beginning of it so well, that for the sake of that, I tacked to it the respectably-tame conclusion. I have no objection, as you have been pleased with it, to restore the whole piece. Could you improve it a little?

To the Cuckow. [II, 207]
At once far off and near.

Restore this. The alteration was made, in consequence of my noticing one day, that the voice of a cuckoo, which I had heard from a tree at a great distance, did not seem any louder when I approached the tree.

Gipsies. [II, 226]

The concluding apology shall be cancelled. 'Goings-on' is precisely the word wanted; but it makes a weak, and apparently prosaic line, so near the end of a poem. I fear it cannot be altered, as the rhyme must be retained, on account of the concluding verse.[58]

In the second 'Cuckoo' [II, 265], I was displeased with the existing alteration and in my copy have written in pencil thus:—

> Such rebounds our inward ear
> Often catches from afar,
> Listen, ponder,   &c.

restoring 'Listen, ponder'. The word 'rebounds' I wish much to

---

[57] See this poem in Chapter V [BF].
[58] I have not a copy of my letter; but I suppose I preferred

> The silent Heavens have goings-on—
> The stars have tasks, but these have none,

to the concluding apology, for which these lines were omitted. The alteration was made in consequence of Mr Coleridge's critique in his Biographia Literaria, vol. ii, p. 153 [Shawcross, Vol. II, p. 110], in which he charges the poet with reflecting that the poor tawny wanderers might probably have been tramping for weeks together, and consequently might have been right glad to rest themselves for one whole day. I believe I replied to this objection, that travelling industry was not the habit of gipsies, who are naturally loitering, basking, idlers,—'taskless' in the strongest sense of the word; and that the poet's moral was truly drawn, though perhaps the contrasted images and thoughts might be too great for the subject [BF]. (Field's letter is given in the Appendix.)

introduce here; for the imaginative warning turns upon the echo, which ought to be revived as near the conclusion as possible.[59]

Peele Castle, in a storm. [IV, 258]

The light that never was, on sea or land,

shall be restored. I need not trouble you with the reasons that put me upon the alteration.

The passages in *Peter Bell* [II, 331] were altered out of deference to the opinions of others. You say *little* is a word of endearment: I meant *little mulish* as contemptuous. *Spiteful*, I fear, would scarcely be understood without your anecdote.

> Is it a party in a parlour?
> Cramm'd just as they on earth were cramm'd—
>> Some sipping punch, some sipping tea,
>> But as you by their faces see,
> All silent, and all damned.

This stanza I omitted, though one of the most imaginative in the whole piece, not to offend the pious.[60]

The Excursion, edit^n of 1827.

And make the vessel of the big round year,

p. 364. [Bk IX, l. 134, V, 291]

---

[59] This rule of art holds equally good, as to the theme of a piece of music, as in a poem.

> Prima dicte, mihi, summa dicende Camoena.—*Horat.* [BF]

This note was printed as part of Wordsworth's letter by Knight in *Letters*, and consequently in de Selincourt, with the reference *Epistolae*, I, i, 1 added.

[60] I entirely acquiesce in the propriety of this motive. Mr Wordsworth had not only an eminent brother, but a son, in the church; and something is surely due to the feelings of such relatives. I therefore protest against the publication, in a recent work, of a confidential letter by Mr Coleridge, in which Mr Wordsworth is suspected of 'wordly prudence carried into religion—at least ⟨says the letter-writer⟩ it conjures up to my fancy a sort of Janus-head of Spinoza and Dr Watts, or *I and my brother the Dean*'. Mr Coleridge would have bitterly regretted, had he lived to see this letter in print. It was the mere transient fancy of a disappointed moment. It was written before the postscript to Mr Wordsworth's Yarrow Revisited [II, 444-62], containing a defence of the inequalities in the remuneration of our clergy, which I wish he had never published, but which is sophisticated and paradoxical enough for Mr Coleridge to have agreed in [BF]. This note is lengthened for B. Coleridge's letter to Thomas Allsop of 8 August 1820, *Letters*, V, 93-7, was published in *Letters, Conversations & Recollections of S. T. Coleridge*, ed. T. Allsop, 1836, p. 54.

I know there is such a line as this somewhere; but for the life of me, I cannot tell where.[61]

> He yielded, tho' reluctant, for his mind
> Instinctively dispos'd him to retire
> To his own covert; as a billow heav'd
> Upon the beach, rolls back into the sea.
>
> p. 192. [Bk V, ll. 75-8, V, 155]

I cannot accede to your objection to the billow. The point simply is, he was cast out of his element; and falls back into it, as naturally and necessarily as a billow into the sea. There is imagination in fastening solely upon that characteristic point of resemblance, stopping there, thinking of nothing else.

> And there,
> Merrily seated in a ring partook,
> The beverage drawn from China's fragrant herb.
>
> p. 380. [Bk IX, ll. 528-30 var., V, 304]

'Drank tea' is too familiar. My line is (I own) somewhat too pompous, as you say.[62] I am much pleased that you think the alterations of the Excursion improvements. My sister thinks them so invariably.[63] Read page 332 thus:

---

[61] I have never been able to find such a line, in all my (too great) poetical reading. Shakspeare has

Fills the wide vessel *of the universe,*

in King Henry the Fifth, and 'the big round *tears*' in As You Like It [BF]. As de Selincourt notes (V, 472), Wordsworth altered 'vessel' to 'chalice' because Field objected that 'vessel' was ambiguous. See Field's letter in Appendix.

[62] It now stands—

A choice repast—serv'd by our young companions,
With rival earnestness and kindred glee.   [BF]

Printed as part of Wordsworth's letter by Knight and de Selincourt, cf. n. 59.

[63] I would except only the following alteration: The line, which resumes the narrative, after the noble effusion, which is quoted at the conclusion of the 10th Chapter of this little work, stood in the first edition:—

No apter strain could have been chosen: I mark'd—

It is now—

As this apt strain proceeded, I could mark—

I remember to have heard the poet, one evening at Mr Lamb's, read the whole passage with his usual unction; and, himself condemning the harshness of the original line, he altered it to

Though apprehensions cross'd me that my zeal
To his might well be liken'd, &c.

[Bk VIII, ll. 21-2, V, 266]

shorter. Page 220, for 'when night' &c. read 'till night' &c. [Bk V, l. 766, V, 177]

I remain very faithfully your's,
W. Wordsworth.[64]

The whole of this letter is too valuable, as a lecture upon the art of poetry, to be lost. 'Such is the labour ⟨as Dr Johnson says⟩ of those who write for immortality'. I think it proves that there was a considerable difference between the poet's theory,[W][65] and his practice; as I shall show more at large in a subsequent chapter [Ch. VIII].

The passage on similes in the letter taught me a lesson in poetry, namely, that in the higher regions of imagination, and above all, when the simile or metaphor comes from the lips of passion, partial resemblance is sufficient; but in didactic or lighter poetry, the resemblance should have more points. The following very perfect and beautiful simile will illustrate this. It was written when W. Wordsworth was less than twenty years old.

Alas! the idle tale of Man is found,
Depicted on the Dial's moral round . . .
He knows but from its shade the present hour.

['An Evening Walk', 1793, ll. 37-42, I, 6]

But this species of fancy must not be carried so far as to become a mere conundrum, like Dr Young's 'Why is the opera like a pillory?' [Field here has a discussion of 'sufficient simile'. He opposes the views of Lowth, Lamb, Dr Johnson, Boileau, Warton and Hazlitt, and uses

---

The strain was aptly chosen: I could mark—

for the sake of the pause in the middle of the line, which was a relief after the full period of the preceding lines, ending

The simple shepherd's awe-inspiring god.

We all thought this a great improvement, and a learned harmony. Why was the short pause thrown away again? [BF]. The slight variant is not noted in de Selincourt. The 'evening at Lamb's' was possibly 23 May 1815 when Wordsworth was 'very chatty on poetry', Field's first or second meeting with the poet. *Henry Crabb Robinson on Books and their Writers*, ed. Morley, 3 vols, London 1938, Vol. I, p. 167.

[64] 'Read p. 332 thus. . . . "till night" &c.' not in Knight's *Letters* and consequently not in de Selincourt.

[65] **I reserve what I have to say upon this word** *theory* **till I have the pleasure of seeing you** [WW].

Wordsworth, Young, Cowper, Bowles, Waller, Collins, Campbell and Barry Cornwall to provide examples. Apart from Wordsworth, he approves only of Bowles and Waller. The discussion is steered round to Wordsworth's letter to Field of 20 December 1828, *Letters, Later Years*, I, 340-1, which is quoted from 'I am truly glad you liked the "Triad" [II, 292-8] . . .' The letter includes, 'I should like to write a short Indian piece, if you would furnish me with a story. Southey mentioned one to me in Forbes's Travels in India. Have you access to the book, and leisure to consult it? He has it not. It is of a Hindoo girl, who applied to a Bramin to recover a faithless lover . . .']

I had not access to Forbes's Oriental Memoirs at that time;[66] but I sent the poet the fine story from that book, quoted in the Quarterly Review, of the Bramin who had been shown in a solar microscope the innumerable animalculae, which he ate upon all the vegetable food, to which he thought he confined himself. The Bramin became thoughtful, bought the microscope, precipitated it to pieces, and addressed his friend:— 'Oh, that I had remained in that happy state of ignorance, in which you found me! Yet I confess that, as my knowledge increased, so did my pleasure, till I beheld the wonders of the microscope: from that moment I have been tormented with doubts. I am miserable, and must continue to be so, till I enter upon another stage of existence. I am a solitary individual among fifty millions of people, all brought up in the same belief as myself, and all happy in their ignorance. I will keep the secret within my own bosom: it will destroy my peace; but I shall have some satisfaction in knowing that I alone feel those doubts, which, had I not destroyed the instrument, might have been communicated to others, and rendered thousands wretched. Forgive me, my friend, and bring here no more instruments of knowledge.'

To this communication I received the following answer[s] . . .[67]

After ten years, alas! as one of my old friends addresses me,

> Me procul a patria retinet Tartossia Calpe

But I still live in hopes to

> grasp the hand again,
> That gave the British Harp its truest sound.[68]

[66] James Forbes, *Oriental Memoirs* . . ., 4 vols, London 1813. Field identifies the passage as 'vol. iii, pp. 233-5', and reproduces it in a long note as one 'which has so narrowly escaped from being married to "immortal verse"'.

[67] Letters of 19 January and 26 February 1829, *Letters, Later Years*, I, 346-7, 382. The latter is not dated in Knight or de Selincourt and the penultimate sentence, 'I write this note, as an affectionate farewell', omitted.

[68] Landor, 'Ode to a Friend', *Poetical Works*, Vol. III, p. 9. Field repeats the lines from the Dedication.

[Chapter III ended at this point in A. In B Field continues with the following paragraphs, introduced by a few lines from Montgomery[69] and by the comment that it was eleven years (after Wordsworth's letter of 26 February 1829) before he could 'grasp the hand again'.]

[In 1840, I revisited Rydal Mount. I saw the immortalised 'Portrait': the Poet did me the favour to read his ['Lines suggested by a Portrait from the Pencil of F. Stone', IV, 120-5], while I fed my soul by gazing on their verification. He also read to me in manuscript his Lines on hearing the Cuckoo at the Monastery of San Francisco d'Assisi ['The Cuckoo at Laverna', III, 218], and his modernization of Chaucer's Cuckow & Nightingale [IV, 217-28]. The former is very long and happy: in illustration of the latter, he referred to the part the Crow plays in the Manciple's Tale, and praised the father-poet's dramatic skill and courage, in making the Manciple, whose only object in life was to be a trusty domestic, draw this moral alone from the story:—

> My sone, beware, and be non auctour newe
> Of tidings, whether they ben false or trewe:
> Wher so thou come, amonges high or lowe,
> Kepe wel thy tonge, and thinke upon the Crowe.

He wished that the delicacy of modern ears would allow him to translate the whole of this Tale, and dwelt with rapture upon the remorse of Phoebus for having slain his adulterous wife—

> For sorwe of which he brake his minstralcie,
> Both harpe and lute, giterne and sauterie,
> And eke he brake his arwes and his bowe.

In the year 1841, the poet threw his Cuckow and Nightingale into a bad collection of pieces entitled 'Chaucer Modernized', by Mr Horne,[70] in which Mr Leigh Hunt attempted this Manciple's Tale, by softening the adultery into a kiss, and thus emasculating the whole moral. It is but justice, however, to that gentleman (in early life my friend) to say that his other modernizations of the old poet were worthy to be published with Mr Wordsworth's.

The neighbourhood of Rydal Mount illustrated the poems I had lived upon at Gibraltar. The Garden, the Terrace, the Lake, the very House, breathed of the six volumes. On the mantel-piece of my bedroom was the 'Needle Case in the form of a Harp' [II, 152-3], made by one of the then Laureate's daughters [Edith Southey]. The 'Australian parrot' and the 'gold and silver Fish' were dead; but one

---

[69] 'Meet Again', ll. 1, 9-12, *Poetical Works*, 4 vols, London 1841, Vol. III, p. 208.
[70] R. H. Horne, *The Poems of Geoffrey Chaucer, Modernized*, London 1841.

of the 'Turtle Doves' [II, 155, IV, 151-3, II, 163] survived. The weather
was fine. We strolled over the 'old poetic mountains'.[71] The poet told
me the story of his life, particularly of his acquaintance with Mr
Hazlitt and Mr De Quincey, and of the several causes of the cessation
of these acquaintanceships, unfit to be recorded in writing. He took
me to his early residence in Grasmere, and showed me that

> little nook of mountain-ground,
> Thou rocky corner in the lowest stair
> Of that magnificent temple, which doth bound
> One side of our whole vale with grandeur rare,
> Sweet garden-orchard!
>
> Here thronged with primroses, the steep rock's breast
> Glitter'd at evening, like a starry sky;
> And in this bush our sparrow built her nest,
> Of which I sang one Song that will not die.
>
> ['A Farewell', ll. 1-5, 53-6, II, 23, 25]

It was the season of the celandine and the daffodil, the poet's own
flowers: they were both there, or at Rydal. In the Grasmere Orchard,
I fancied I saw

> that one upright twig,
> That look'd up at the sky so proud and so big
> All last summer, as well you know,
> Studded with apples, a beautiful show!
>
> ['Address to a Child', ll. 24-7, I, 229]

But the authoress of the poem [Dorothy], from which these latter
words are quoted, I did not then see. For her,

> Dread powers, that work in mystery, had spun
> Entanglings for the brain, and shadows stretch'd
> O'er the chilled heart.
>
> ['Oh what a Wreck . . .', ll. 2-4, III, 56-7]

In return, I had the pleasure of becoming acquainted with 'Joanna',
Mrs Wordsworth's sister. And, lastly, I then first saw the Stone in the
grounds of Rydal, in which the following Inscription is inserted,
engraved on a brass plate:—

[71] Gray [BF]. 'The Progress of Poesy', l. 73, *Poems*, ed. H. W. Starr and J. R.
Hendrickson, Oxford 1966, p. 12.

In those fair Vales, hath many a tree
  At Wordsworth's suit been spar'd;
And from the builder's hand this Stone,
  For some rude beauty of its own,
Was rescued by the Bard.

So let it rest; and time will come
  When here the tender-hearted
May heave a gentle sigh for him
  As one of the departed.

[IV, 201]

  In the autumn of 1841, I quitted Gibraltar, and spent a few months
in the neighbourhood of the poet, when I had the pleasure of witnessing
his kindness to the 'second childishness' of his own Sister, but not
'mere oblivion' for she recollected me after an interval of fourteen
years. I found the poet's mind still full of the subject of copyright, my
friend Talfourd's bill having been lost the preceding Session, mainly
by the influence of a speech from Mr Macauley [*sic*], which had
asserted among other extravagancies, that if copyright had been of
longer duration, Richardson's son would have suppressed his father's
novels, from religious scruples. The poet was then engaged in com-
municating arguments to the Editor of the Quarterly Review,[72] for an
article on the subject, which appeared in the number for December
following; and as I had, in early life, known this descendant of
Richardson, I assisted Mr Wordsworth by contributing the following
paragraph to that article:—

> The grandson (not *son*) of Richardson to whom he alludes, was the Rev.
> Samuel Crowther, vicar of Christ Church, in London, a most worthy man,
> and of some note as what is called 'an evangelical preacher'. In a note to his
> funeral sermon, his friend Daniel Wilson (now the exemplary Bishop of
> Calcutta) made the statement on which alone Mr Macaulay had to rely—it
> is in these words:—'Mr C. once said, in a humorous way, I am an unworthy
> grandson never to have read those celebrated works.' Does it follow that
> Mr Crowther would have suppressed them without first reading them, or
> that, if he had read them, he would have been willing to suppress them at
> all? But he was only one of several sons of one of Richardson's daughters:
> other daughters also left sons; and even Mr Crowther's own brother, the
> surgeon of Bethlehem Hospital, was a man of habits and tastes totally
> different from his. In no case, therefore, could the Rev. Vicar have had the
> power to keep back a new edition of the Clarissa even for a single year.

Lord Mahon, who took up the subject next Session, upon Mr Serjeant
Talfourd's retirement from the House, also made use of this fact in his

[72] See *Notes and Queries*, CCX, pp. 411-13.

Speech. His lordship's bill proposed that copyright should hereafter continue for the author's life and twenty-five years longer. Mr Macauley, strange to say, after his last year's Speech, concurred in the objects of the proposed measure, but thought they would be better accomplished by granting protection for the author's life, *or* for forty-two years, whichever should be the longer term. Sir Robert Peel declared himself in favour of Mr Macauley's amendment, but proposed to give an additional seven years, in case the author should survive the 42 years; and Mr Macauley's proposition, with Sir Robert's improvement, was carried; and the bill thus became law.

In the same number of the Quarterly Review, were published 14 Sonnets on the proposed abolition of capital punishment for murder [IV, 135-41], the first of which I had the honour, in 1840, of suggesting to the poet, by telling him the little fact on which it is founded. 'Thank you for that', said he at the time, and no more. The story bred silently with his profound thoughts on the subject; and in 1841 he read me the whole series of these jurisprudent reasonings, worthy of Verulam.

Soon afterwards, in 1842, was published the poet's seventh volume, comprehending these Sonnets, entitled 'Poems, chiefly of early and late years, including the Borderers, a tragedy'. The curiosity of his friends had always been so great, to read this drama; but I only speak the universal opinion, when I say that we were disappointed. Like all tragedies, that hinge upon false testimony, and exposure to starvation, the Borderers is an irritating and incredible drama. In its metaphysics, it reminds us forcibly that it was written in communion with Mr Coleridge's 'Remorse'. Like everything else of Mr Wordsworth's, it is full of thought and poetry; but it leaves us quite satisfied of the author's judgment in having withheld its publication, till it should be interesting only as a part of the history of his genius.]

CHAPTER IIII   In private life (and Mr Wordsworth's whole life is private, for early mountain-retirement was essential to his lofty poetic moods) the poet is one of the most amiable of men, and lives devoted to his family. His maiden sister, Dorothy, the authoress of four of the poems in his collection, and the companion of his earlier travels, lived with that family; and is thus alluded to in one of his poems:

> The blessing of my later years
>   Was with me when a boy;
> She gave me eyes, she gave me ears—
>   A heart the fountain of sweet tears,
> And love and thought and joy.

['The Sparrow's Nest', ll. 15-19, I, 227]

Mr Wordsworth's elder brother, Mr Richard Wordsworth, was a Solicitor in London, but he died early, leaving one son; the third brother was[W73] Capt. John Wordsworth who perished in the wreck of the Earl of Abergavenny East Indiaman, off the coast of Dorsetshire. He forms the subject of one of the poet's most beautiful epitaphs ['Elegiac Verses . . .', IV, 263-5].

The following extract from an anonymous Tour, published in Mr Hone's Table-book (1828)[74] will show that Mr Wordsworth's sympathies with the poor were

> not conjured up
> To serve occasions of poetic pomp,
> But genuine.[75]

'I had scarcely reached the village of Rydal, when a shower drove me into a cottage, from the door of which I had my first view of the author of the Lyrical Ballads. He is rather tall, apparently about fifty years of age: he was dressed in a hairy cap, plaid coat and white trowsers. It was gratifying to hear how the Rydal peasantry spoke of this good man. One said he was kind to the poor; another that he was very religious; a third that he had no pride, and would speak to anybody: all were loud in his praise.'

And so Mrs Hemans writes from Rydal Mount in 1830:—
'I am charmed with Mr Wordsworth, whose kindness to me has quite a soothing influence over my spirits. Oh, what relief, what blessing there is, in the feeling of admiration, when it can be freely poured forth!

> There is a daily beauty in his life,

which is in such lovely harmony with his poetry, that I am thankful to have witnessed it and felt it * * * * * * * You will be pleased to hear that the more I see of Mr Wordsworth, the more I admire, and I may almost say love, him. It is delightful to see a life in such perfect harmony with all that his writings express.

> True to the kindred points of Heav'n and Home.

You may remember how much I disliked, and I think you agreed with me in reprobating, that shallow theory of Mr Moore's, in his

---

[73] Wordsworth has made minor corrections to avoid a possible impression that there were four brothers.
[74] William Hone, *The Table Book*, 2 vols, London 1827, 1828, 'Notes on a Tour', Vol. II, cols. 271-83, signed 'T.Q.M.'
[75] William Cowper, *The Task*, Bk I, ll. 151-3, *Poetical Works*, ed. H. S. Milford, Oxford 1934, p. 132.

Life of Lord Byron, with regard to the unfitness of genius for domestic happiness. I was speaking of it yesterday to Mr Wordsworth, and was pleased with his remark:— "It is not because they possess genius that they make unhappy homes, but because they do not possess genius enough. A higher order of mind would enable them to see and feel all the beauty of domestic ties." He has himself been singularly fortunate in long years of almost untroubled domestic peace and union.'[76]

[The first paragraph below in A only, and crossed through; the second in B only; the third added to A for B.]

[Since the settlement in life of his three children, Mount Rydal has generally been full of female guests and inmates; the following inscription is the elegant Dedication of Madame Françoise Trembicke's [sic] Mémoires d'Une Polonaise, pour servir a l'histoire de la Pologne depuis 1765 jusqu' à 1830:— 'à William Wordsworth Esq. offert par l'auteur à l'un des premiers poètes de l'Angleterre, à l'excellent homme dont la poésie servit à exprimer les sentimens bienveillans de son âme, ce faible hommage est dicté par le désir de donner quelque durée au souvenir des momens écoulés à Mount-Rydal. Paris, le 25 Mai, 1841.'[77]

Having paid my humble tribute to the many virtues, both personal and literary, of this great Poet, not even this biographical Sketch can be considered as impartial and complete, without some indications of shadow in the composition. But the only failing, with which I am acquainted, in Mr Wordsworth, was a turning away from the works of his contemporaries, and too constant a concentration of his regards upon his own poems. I shall not condescend to repeat or to record the anecdotes, upon this subject, true or false, as to the poems of Southey, which Lord Byron has maliciously printed, and as to the novel of Rob Roy, which I think I have read in the newspapers; but I shall admit that one of the poet's few weaknesses was a disinclination to know and appreciate the poems of his living brethren. He was somewhat jealous even of his disciples and imitators. He read not many; and was engrossed with his own thoughts and effusions, which he loved to read aloud, to talk of, and to polish. But to the young and struggling poet, how exquisite would have been the occasional encouragement of a word from his pen! And how fervent was the practice, in this respect, of his friends, Scott, Southey, Coleridge and Lamb! But if he neglected his contemporaries, he was familiar with

---

[76] Henry F. Chorley, *Memorials of Mrs Hemans*, 2 vols, London 1836, Vol. II, pp. 116-7, 119-20. The quoted lines are *Othello*, V, i, 19 (which is remarkably inappropriate) and 'To a Skylark', l. 12, II, 266.

[77] Françoise Trembicka, *Mémoires d'Une Polonaise* . . . 2 vols, Paris 1841. There is no other mention of Wordsworth or Rydal Mount, but the Introduction suggests she lived for some years in England.

the poems of predecessors, although I think (as is often the case with
artists of genius) he preferred such as he, at first sight, least resembled,
for instance, Pope . . .

Mr Wordsworth is no book-collector; but he possesses the earliest
editions of Milton, Dryden, Pope, Thomson, Akenside, Collins, Gray,
&c., some of them with the subsequent alterations in MS. These
comparisons afford the best of all studies of the art of poetry and it is
very curious to have in one's hand the little volume of Collins's Odes,
of which he destroyed all the unsold copies from mortification at their
non-sale; and the copy of Gray's Elegy, of which, when the proof of
the *cul-de-lampe* was sent him, while in the company of his Aunts, they
asked him, from its black borders of skulls and hour-glasses, whether
he had got a ticket for somebody's burying. 'Heaven forbid ⟨adds
Gray⟩ that they should suspect it to belong to any verses of mine;
they would burn me for a poet.'[78]]

Mr Wordsworth's patrimony was small, and at the time when he
published his earlier poems, the fair profits of authorship would have
been an acceptable addition to it. But it was the wit of the new
Edinburgh Review and not the dulness of the old Monthly that
prevented the public from purchasing his works.

The poet having now taken his niche for ever in the Temple of
Fame, and his foaming reviewer having subsided into a forensic judge,
it may afford an useful lesson to both authors and critics, at this
distance of time, to look back calmly and dispassionately upon the
history of this case, and then to close the 'old almanack' of the
Edinburgh Review for ever. Mr Wordsworth's Lyrical Ballads were
published before the institution of this literary inquisition; but their
preface was commented upon in the very first number of the Review,
and upon the appearance of the poet's two miscellaneous volumes in
1807, the tribunal acquired legal jurisdiction of the whole author, and
from that time did this critical journal effectually prevent the public
from judging of his works for itself. It was necessary to the sale of that
review, that authors should be ridiculed, and readers flattered that they
were wiser than authors, and almost as wise as reviewers. In his
pamphlet concerning Burns, and in the introductory paragraph to his
Supplement to his celebrated Preface, which paragraph he since
suppressed,[79] Mr Wordsworth has been accused of bitterness towards

[78] *Correspondence*, ed. P. Toynbee and L. Whibley, 3 vols, Oxford, rev. ed.
H. W. Starr, 1971, Vol. II, p. 362 (8 July 1752).
[79] *Letter to a Friend of Robert Burns*, 1816, *Prose Works*, ed. A. B. Grosart, 3 vols,
London 1876, Vol. II, pp. 1-19. In 1815 the Essay Supplementary opened, 'By
this time, I trust that the judicious Reader, who has now first become acquainted
with these poems, is persuaded that a very senseless outcry has been raised

his critics; but it must be borne in mind that severity of rebuke was
then necessary from English bards towards Scotch reviewers. Mr
Jeffrey had absolutely run-a-muck in criticism.[80] His kreess had
stabbed not only Wordsworth, Southey, Coleridge, Lamb, James
Montgomery, Bowles, Moore and Byron, but (to show his un-
nationality and freedom from all sorts of amiable partiality) Burns and
Scott. Nobody was a poet but Campbell, Crabbe and the Author of
the Paradise of Coquettes![81]

> Nul n'aura de l'esprit hors nous et nos amis.
> Molière.

The critic lived to change his tone towards Moore and Byron being
influential anti-tories;[82] but he has never made, and can never make,
any reparation for the injury he did at the time to the fortune and
fame of Mr Wordsworth.[83] The Review was instituted upon the
principles of ridicule and abuse; and the quarterly immolation of a
poet was necessary to console the anti-imaginative taste of the critics
and their readers.

---

against them and their Author. . . . By what fatality the orb of my genius (for
genius none of them seem to deny me) acts upon these men like the moon
upon a certain description of patients, it would be irksome to inquire; nor
would it consist with the respect which I owe myself to take further notice
of opponents whom I internally despise'. See Paul M. Zall, *Literary Criticism
of William Wordsworth*, Lincoln 1966, pp. 158-9, for full paragraph not in de
Selincourt, Knight or Grosart.

[80] The conclusion of his critique on Burns is almost personally contemptuous of
Mr Wordsworth. It is quite comedy to read that the critic's first objection to
Burns is 'the undisciplined harshness and acrimony of his invective' [BF].

[81] Thomas Brown, *Paradise of Coquettes*, London 1814.

[82] We afterwards find Mr Moore turning the spit of the same Review to roast
a succeeding young poet, Lord Thurlow, whose volume contained some of
the most beautiful Sonnets in the language [BF].

[83] The Review is now in other hands; and in the number for July 1840 we find
Mr Wordsworth quoted not by name but as 'the greatest of living poets'. But
in collecting his Critiques for republication in 1843, the following is the only
modification which Lord Jeffrey thought proper to make:— 'I have spoken in
many places rather too bitterly and confidently of the faults of W. Wordsworth's poetry: and forgetting, that, even on my own view of them, they
were but faults of taste, or venial self-partiality, have sometimes visited them,
I fear, with an asperity which should be reserved for objects of moral reproba-
tion. . . . I have always loved many of the attributes of his Genius. . . . [But as]
I still retain in substance the opinions which I should now like to have seen
more gently expressed, I felt that, to omit all notice of him on the present
occasion, might be held to import a retraction which I am as far as possible
from intending . . .' [BF, added for B]. Francis Jeffrey, *Contributions to the
Edinburgh Review*, 4 vols, London 1844, Vol. III, p. 233, headnote to review
of *The Excursion*.

For when a poet now himself doth show,
As if he were a common Foe,
All draw upon him, all around,
And every part of him they wound;
Happy the man that gives the deepest blow.[84]

Poetry had need to be its own exceeding great reward; for little other reward does the poet receive.

There is a pleasure in poetic pains,
Which only poets know ...
But oh! not such,
Or seldom such, the hearers of his Song!
Fastidious, or else listless, or perhaps
Aware of nothing arduous in a task,
They never undertook.[85]

The motto of the Edinburgh Review is

Judex damnatur, cum nocens absolvitur;

as if the employment of paper-makers and printers, binders and booksellers, in publishing a volume, which nobody is compelled to purchase, were a crime, and the harmless author a moral delinquent. What is there in offering a book for sale, more than in giving it away, that should render the former act a public offence, and the latter an innocent deed? Publishing and selling, as every bookseller knows, are two very different things. Of some books, thus advertized, or exposed for sale, not half a dozen copies are sold; and the reviewer's copy is generally a gift. Then where is the crime? What mischief has been done? We have seen, from Mr Cottle's narrative, that of the first edition of the Lyrical Ballads not two hundred copies[W][86] were sold; and the price was not more than two or three shillings for each copy. Of the numbers of the second edition we are not informed. Mr

[84] Cowley, 'Ode upon occasion of a Copy of Verses of my Lord Broghill's', st. 2, *Poems*, Vol. I, pp. 406-7.
[85] Cowper, *The Task*, Bk II, ll. 285-6, 304-8, *Poetical Works*, p. 152.
[86] **The rest were turned over to Arch & must have been sold, before liberty to reprint could be granted. The 2d Edn appeared in 1802** [WW]. Presumably later, prompted by Wordsworth's notes to look again at Cottle, Field has altered his sentence to read, 'of the first edition of the Lyrical Ballads not more than five hundred copies were printed; and the price was only five shillings for each copy and the greater part of them was transferred to another publisher at a loss'. 'What mischief has been done?' is crossed through and replaced by ll. 189-92 from Pope's 'Imitations of Horace, Bk II, Ep. I', *Poetical Works*, ed. Herbert Davis, London 1966, p. 366.

Wordsworth attributed their nonsale to the unintelligibility of Mr Coleridge's Antient Mariner and Mr Coleridge to the paradoxicalness of Mr Wordsworth's preface.[87] Mr Jeffrey admits the justice of such an essoign as nonsale, in his review of Mr Montgomery's Poems, where he says:— 'A third edition is too alarming to be passed over in silence'. But the volumes of Mr Wordsworth's poems, which were then reviewed by Mr Jeffrey, had never gone beyond the first edition. No matter. Whenever the critic had a mind to show his own wit, or to gratify his readers' spleen, *guilty of publishing only* was verdict enough, and sentence of death was immediately passed, lest the judge himself should be condemned to the like destruction. The consequence of this false principle was that the critic concerned himself not so much with the presence of beauties in a composition, as with the absence of faults. The Paradise of Coquettes may (for anything I know of it) be a faultless poem. But nobody ever reads it. I know there are beauties in the earlier poems of Wordsworth, James Montgomery, Lamb, Moore and Byron; but Mr Jeffrey conceived that his trade was to extract and ridicule the faults of those poems, or what he considered as such. The business of a state-judge is only with faults or crimes: it is *his* part to be a terror to evil doers, and it is not often that he can be even a praise to them that do well. *He* may be to blame, when the guilty are acquitted; but even with him, the maxim is that it is better that ten guilty should escape, than that one innocent man should be condemned. But a philosophical critic should glory in feeling excellence where it exists, and if it does not exist, the book is beneath the notice of a review like our quarterly journals, which were instituted upon the principle of selection of eminence; and the obscure volume may be safely suffered to expire, at the expense of nobody but the author. This remark applies more particularly to the critiques in the Edinburgh Review upon Lamb, James Montgomery and Lord Byron. Their early volumes were pronounced to be utterly worthless, and ought therefore not to have been noticed. Mr Moore was allowed to have some talents; but he was treated rather as a moral delinquent—a charge to which some of his poems laid him too open. The ridicule of Mr Wordsworth was purely literary, and it was alledged that the great Ode, since entitled 'Intimations of Immortality from recollections of early Childhood', which now ranks with the lyric master-pieces of Dryden, Collins Gray and Akenside (say above them) was, 'beyond all doubt, the most illegible and unintelligible part of the publication'.

[87] **My observations on the Ancient Mariner attached only to the first Ed when the Preface had not appeared** [WW]. Field altered his sentence to read, 'the nonsale of the first edition . . . Antient Mariner without the Preface and Mr Coleridge that of the second to the paradoxicalness . . .'

And as dogs bark at those they do not know,
So they at such they do not understand.

Daniel

I have no doubt that this poem was unintelligible to such a critic; and
yet he did not want a head: few men in the world were gifted with
such wit and mental acuteness: he only wanted a heart . . .[88]

To proceed;—The Edinburgh Review next admitted that Mr
Wordsworth could write good verses when he pleased, and contended
that he always did write good verses, when he was led to abandon his
system. The Song on the restoration of Lord Clifford was then quoted,
as an instance of this, together with three Sonnets, and the critic
admitted that there were many still finer passages.[89] Should not the
poet then have been forgiven for the sake of these? Is not 'a dram of
sweet worth a pound of sour'?[90] Mr Jeffrey

—saw, not felt, how beautiful they were.
It were a vain endeavour,
Though he should gaze for ever,
On that green light that lingers in the west:
He may not hope from outward forms to win
The passion and the life, whose fountains are within:
O Critic! we receive but what we give.[91]

Poetry (as I once heard Mr Coleridge himself say) knocks at the door:
if there is nobody at home, it goes away . . .[92]

[88] Field here quotes approvingly passages from Coleridge, Preface to *Poems*, 1797
('An author is obscure when his conceptions are dim. . . . it is more consoling
to our pride to consider him as lost beneath, than as soaring above, us', *Poems*,
Vol. II, p. 1145), from Young ('It is the genuine character, and true merit of
the Ode to startle some apprehensions . . . comfortable mistake, that all is
wrong, which falls not within the narrow limits of their own comprehensions
and relish.'), and from Gray ('Mr Bedingford [Bedingfield] writes me word . . .
but yet thinks they understand them as well as they do Milton and Shakespeare,
whom they are obliged by fashion to admire', *Corr.*, Vol. II, p. 532).
[89] Edinburgh Review, vol. xi, p. 231 [BF].
[90] Spenser [*Faery Queen*, I, iii, 30, 4]. [BF]. Field has later inserted here a passage
from the 'Edinburgh Review, vol. vij, p. 295', in which Jeffrey quotes Hallam to
the effect that the pleasures of a cultivated taste greatly exceed the pains which
may correspond to them, so that while there is keen delight in reading an
excellent poem, the uneasiness of reading a bad one is trifling. Field's point is
that Jeffrey could not profit by the lesson.
[91] Cf. Coleridge's 'Dejection: an Ode', ll. 38-47, *Poems*, Vol. I, pp. 364-5.
[92] Field here inserts a line from Goëthe, tr. as: 'Who would the Poet understand
Must enter first the Poet's land'. He continues with a passage from the *British
and Foreign Review* to the effect that the vague, as distinct from the obscure,
claims a quarter of every powerful poetic impression, leading the soul to
compose its own poetry; this, Field implies, Jeffrey did not recognise.

If the heart of the Edinburgh Reviewer had really been touched by these many fine passages in Mr Wordsworth's poems, ought not compassion, rather than scorn, to have been the result? The public taste will always be much more benefitted by the analysis and exposition of beautiful poetry, than by the ridicule of deformed.

> The generous critic fann'd the poet's fire,
> And taught the world with reason to admire.[93]

The reader should be excited to imitate, or at least to taste and feel, excellence, and not flattered that he has, by never committing the sin of publication, avoided failure—'that he is not like this publican'.[94]

But the climax of Mr Jeffrey's injustice to Mr Wordsworth is to be found in his review of the 'Rejected Addresses', in which he says that the authors of that book have, in their burlesque called The Baby's Debût, 'succeeded perfectly in the imitation of the poet's mawkish affectations of childish simplicity and nursery stammering'.[95] Is then the Excursion, as Sophocles said of his Oedipus Coloneus, the work of a childish or silly person? Is the White Doe of Rylstone—that 'drop of history ⟨as old Fuller has it⟩ blown by Fancy into a bubble of poetry'? The writer of the *jeu d'esprit* in question has long been of a very different opinion from his reviewer. He, like hundreds of others, knew nothing of Mr Wordsworth's poetry then, but what he had read in the Edinburgh Review itself; but he has since done noble justice to one who is now his favorite poet. In the preface to the last edition of the Rejected Addresses, we read:— 'To raise a harmless laugh was our main object, in the attainment of which we were sometimes hurried into extravagance. In no instance were we thus betrayed into a greater injustice than in the case of Mr Wordsworth—the touching sentiment, profound wisdom, and copious harmony of whose loftier writings we left unnoticed, in the despair of burlesquing them, while we pounced upon his popular ballads, and excited ourselves to push their simplicity into puerility and silliness. With pride and pleasure do we now claim to be ranked among the most ardent admirers of this true poet. And if he himself could see the state of his works, which are ever at our right hand, he would perhaps receive the manifest evidences they exhibit of constant reference and delighted reperusal, as some sort of *amende honorable* for the unfairness of which we were guilty, when we were less conversant with the higher inspirations of his Muse'.[96]

[93] Pope, *Essay on Criticism*, ll. 100-1, *Poetical Works*, p. 67. A remark from Goëthe 'When I have called the bad bad, what is gained by that?' inserted for B.

[94] Luke xviij, 11. [BF in B]. Presumably a pun is intended.

[95] Edinburgh Review vol. xx, p. 438 [BF].

[96] Horace and James Smith, *Rejected Addresses . . .*, London 1833 edn., pp. xii xiii, slightly misquoted. See also Field's letter of 10 April 1828, in Appendix.

Mr Wordsworth was never offended with this professed caricature, as he justly was with Mr Jeffrey's critical injustice; but he once observed to me that the Mr Smiths, if their imitation was, as Mr Jeffrey asserted, 'a very fair and even flattering one of Alice Fell, and the greater part of his last volumes', should have printed Alice Fell itself in their book, just as the authors of the celebrated Probationary Odes for the Laureateship, as if in despair of making Tom Warton more ridiculous than he had made himself, when they came to his turn, gave, instead of a parody or burlesque, a real laureate Ode by Warton himself . . .[97]

In the Monthly Review of Mr Wordsworth's poems, there is a singular betrayal of the envious feelings, in which such critiques as Mr Jeffrey's originate. After quoting a passage from the poet's preface, the critic says:— 'We are so thoroughly overwhelmed by the high and mighty tone of this author's prose, that we really must have recourse to his verse, in order to get rid of the painful humiliation and sense of inferiority, that he inflicts on his readers. There (*Dieu merci!*) we are comforted by silliness, instead of system, by want of harmony, instead of abundance of pride, by downright vacancy instead of grandeur and presumption'.[W98] So that silliness, want of harmony and downright vacancy, (to say nothing of their hated and humiliating opposites, system, pride and grandeur) instead of being failings to lament and deplore in an author, are comforts to congenial dulness—things for reviewers to thank God for' . . .[99]

There never was a falser maxim than that in Boileau's Art of Poetry:—

> Un sonnet sans défauts vaut seul un long poème.

Faultlessness is not beauty or excellence. A long poem, if it be really a poem, though full of faults, is of more value than many faultless sonnets—multis passeribus melior. 'A long poem ⟨as Mr Coleridge says⟩ neither can, nor ought to be all poetry.' Shakspeare will have his unequal scenes, the Paradise Lost its flat, and the Excursion its heavy, passages; but none but a Rymer, a Johnson or a Jeffrey, would

---

[97] Joseph Richardson *et al.*, *Probationary Odes for the Laureateship* . . . by Sir John Hawkins, Knt, London 1785; Warton's Ode on p. 57. Field continues with a brief digression on parody and self-parody illustrated from Byron.

[98] Monthly Review for November, 1815 [BF]. **All this extract is now read by me for the first time** [WW].

[99] Field here has passages on the distinction between honest and fault-finding criticism from 'Scriblerus' and Dryden's Preface to *The State of Innocence*.

criticize the respective poems from their faults, and not from their beauties...[100]

'... In the critical remarks, therefore, prefixed and annexed to the Lyrical Ballads, I believe that we may safely rest, as the true origin of the unexampled opposition, which Mr Wordsworth's writings have been since doomed to encounter. The humbler passages in the poems themselves were dwelt upon and cited to justify the rejection of the theory.[W101] What, in and for themselves, would have been either forgotten or forgiven as imperfections or at least comparative failures, provoked direct hostility, when announced as intentional, as the result of choice, after full deliberation ...'

Let it be permitted to one of the humblest of the 'admirers' here alluded to, to give a reason for the faith that is in him—to show that he has loved the poetry of Wordsworth, 'not too well, but wisely'; and for this purpose to lay his foundations somewhat deeply in the philosophy of poetry and criticism.

CHAPTER V   The four noblest expositions of poetry, in the English language, are those by Sir Philip Sidney, Lord Bacon, Sir William D'Avenant and Milton. Bishop Lowth's Introductory Lecture,[102] which all our Encyclopaedias refer to, is derived from these fountains.

---

[100] Field here has a passage from Addison to the effect that the true critic should dwell upon excellences and discover concealed beauties rather than sourly and easily attack imperfections (*Spectator* no. 291; ed. Donald F. Bond, 5 vols, Oxford 1965, Vol. III, pp. 86-7). It is followed by a long passage from Coleridge (*Biog. Lit.*, Vol. I, pp. 50-5, omitting p. 53, ll. 1-17). Only the sentences attracting Wordsworth's note are given below.

[101] **In the foregoing there is frequent reference to what is called Mr Ws theory, & his Preface. I will mention that I never cared a straw about the theory— & the Preface was written at the request of Mr Coleridge out of sheer good nature. I recollect the very spot, a deserted Quarry in the Vale of Grasmere where he pressed the thing upon me, & but for that it would never have been thought of. I should have written many things like the Essay upon Epitaphs out of kindness to him in the Friend but he always put me off by saying— 'You must wait till my principles are laid down & then I shall be happy to have your contributions.['] But the principles never were laid down & the work fell to the ground. As I never was fond of writing prose & required some incitement to do so, I rather regret having been prevented in this way by my dr Friend** [WW]. Wordsworth has underlined 'In the critical .. encounter'.

[102] Robert Lowth, *Lectures on Hebrew Poetry*, Oxford 1753. Field refers to th 'Introduction: of the uses and design of poetry', which, like the passages h quotes, places poetry above history and philosophy. They quote the sam passage from Bacon.

As they reflect much light on each other, I shall quote them in their order of date.

[In this chapter Field quotes lengthily from *An Apology for Poetry* and more briefly from *The Advancement of Learning*, the Preface to *Gondibert*, and, at the end, Milton's Preface to Edward Phillips's *Theatrum Poetarum*, making practically no comment but setting two lines from Davies of Hereford between the first and second passage, a stanza from Marvell between the second and third, and a critical comment from Addison after Milton's Preface. Field's own contribution to the chapter, still heavy with quotation, comes between the third and fourth extracts. Like the extracts, it concerns a distinction between historical or factual truth and the philosophic or rational truth of poetry. He takes his cue from the last remark in the D'Avenant extract, '... truth, narrative and past, is the idol of historians (who worship a dead thing), and truth, operative and by effects continually alive, is the mistress of poets, who hath not her existence in matter, but in reason'.[103]]

I like that word *reason*. Some criticism may be of opinion that Addison's word, in the following passage, ought to have been fancy, as contra-distinguished from *reality*. He is speaking of the Stars:

> What though no *real* voice or sound,
> Amid their radiant orbs be found,
> In *Reason*'s ear they all rejoice,
> And utter forth a glorious voice,
> For ever singing, as they shine,
> The Hand that made us is divine![104]

It was a happy boldness in the poet not to have said '*fancy*'s ear'. It is the ear of a poet's reason ... [Field here gives examples of addresses to heavenly harmony or the music of the spheres as corresponding to

---

[103] The Sidney passage corresponds to *Elizabethan Critical Essays*, ed. G. Gregory Smith, 2 vols, Oxford 1904, Vol. I, p. 159, ll. 3-24, p. 167, l. 14-p. 168, l. 6, p. 171, ll. 2-24, p. 172, ll. 8-23; the Bacon passage to *Critical Essays of the Seventeenth Century*, ed. J. E. Spingarn, 3 vols, Oxford 1908, Vol. I, p. 6, ll. 1-25; the D'Avenant passage to Spingarn, Vol. II, p. 3, ll. 28-34, p. 10, l. 29-p. 11, l. 11; the Milton passage to Spingarn, Vol. II, p. 267, l. 13-p. 268, l. 6. The Davies lines are, 'Oh! 'tis a sacred kind of excellence, That hides a rich truth in a tale's pretence'; the Marvell stanza ll. 27-32, 'The Picture of little T.C. ...', *Poems and Letters*, ed. H. M. Margoliouth, 2 vols, Oxford 1952, Vol. I, p. 38; the Addison comment from *Spectator* No. 273, Bond, Vol. II, p. 563.
[104] In *Spectator*, No. 465; Bond, Vol. IV, p. 145.

Reason from (in his order) Sidney, Wordsworth, Dyer, Shakespeare, Milton, Keats and Pope.[105]]

Poetry (to parody Shakspeare) is made better by no reason,

> But Fancy makes that reason.
> The reason itself is Fancy.

In poetry, there is no opposition between reason and fancy.[106] Dr Warton writes to Mr Hayley that all he said in his Essay on Pope is comprehended in Mr Hayley's words:— 'He chose to be the poet of reason rather than of fancy'. And this view of Pope's poetry is countenanced by the lines of the poet himself:

> That not in Fancy's maze he wander'd long,
> But stoop'd to Truth, and moraliz'd his song,[107]

which Lord Byron would read 'rose to Truth'. By these lines, Pope meant that he sang metaphysical truth [(that is to say, when he understood it, and did not mistake it) *del*.] and ethics or morals; for all poets must stoop or rise to truth and moralize their songs, however fanciful they may be, and fanciful they must be, to be poets at all. Even Pope's

---

[105] *Astrophel and Stella*, Sixth Song, ll. 49-52, *Poems*, ed. W. A. Ringler, Oxford 1962, p. 217; *The Excursion*, Bk V, ll. 204-07, V, 147-8; *The Fleece*, I, ll. 615-6, *Poems*, ed. Edward Thomas, London 1903, p. 65; *Merchant of Venice*, V, i, 60-5; 'Arcades', ll. 72-3, *Poetical Works*, ed. Douglas Bush, London 1966, p. 103; 'Ode on a Grecian Urn', ll. 11-14, *Poetical Works*, ed. H. W. Garrod, Oxford, 2nd edn 1958, p. 261; *Essay on Man*, I, ll. 201-4, *Poetical Works*, p. 247 Field identifies Keats's 'spirit' as Reason, and agrees with Warburton that in the Pope lines, 'The poet is arguing philosophically in a case that required him to employ the *real* objects of sense only; but if there be no music of the spheres, there was no real sound; which his argument could not do without'.

[106] Nor is there in metaphysics. Reason and fancy must act together. We, popularly speaking, attribute dreams to fancy; but they are merely waking thoughts and sleeping reason; and we might as well dignify the delusions of a lunatic with the name of poetry. In both sleep and madness, there is a suspension of reason; and it is an awful reflexion that for at least one third part of our lives, namely in sleep, we are all mad, as being liable to dream. The lunatic is only a dreamer awake. In both the ideas jumble themselves together, under no controul; but this can never be justly called fancy. Mr Coleridge has written down part of one of his fine dreams in verse, and says that, being interrupted, he lost the rest for ever. But Kubla Khan is a mere rhapsody, and never could have been finished into a fanciful poem; for there is no reason in it. True genius (which includes fancy) is of the highest sanity of mind, as Mr Lamb has shown in his Essay under that title. See Lamb's Prose Works, vol. iii, p. 78 [*Works*, Vol. II, pp. 212-15]. It should seem that reason is the soul, and that that requires sleep as well as the body. The ideas may wake or not. They are only the raw materials of reason [BF].

[107] 'Epistle to Dr. Arbuthnot', ll. 340-1, *Poetical Works*, p. 337.

Essay on Man is full of fancy. The only distinction is between preceptive and exemplary poetry. The preceptive or didactic may (nay must) display fancy, but excludes pathos or passion, except in its episodes; but both kinds must have truth and moral for their object, and imagination or fancy for their means. The exemplary or fictitious poetry has the additional privilege of 'seeking out truth in the passions', as D'Avenant says.

A short poem, more than all others, must have a clear moral, and that moral should be one and entire. The whole poem should tend towards it. Among Mr Wordsworth's poems are two 'To a Skylark', which will exemplify this principle. The first sings out:

> Up with me, up with me! into the clouds,

like the soaring of the bird itself, but its conclusion is lame and inconsequential, like the dropping of the bird to the ground; its moral is so trite, that it can hardly be said to be moralized at all:

> Alas! my journey, rugged and uneven . . .
> And hope for higher raptures, when Life's day is done.
>
> [ll. 1, 26-31, II, 141-2]

The second is a poem indeed. I quote the whole of it.

> Etherial Minstrel! pilgrim of the Sky! . . . .
> True to the kindred points of Heav'n and Home.
>
> [II, 266][108]

Ipsa mollities! That is an exquisite moral, and one to which the argument of the whole poem tends, and the point is concentrated into a happy couplet, which engraves itself on the heart. Cowley had already imagined the following quatrain:—

> The wise example of the heavenly lark,
> Thy fellow-poet, Cowley, mark;
> Above the clouds let thy proud music sound;
> Thy humble nest build on the ground.[109]

But the stanzas of Wordsworth are of so much finer a tissue, as to reduce Cowley's lines to mere prose. The following passage from Mr Hazlitt's 'Spirit of the Age', published in 1825, is much more poetical. Did it suggest to Mr Wordsworth this elegant poem, written

---

[08] Field quotes the 1827 text of three stanzas.
[09] St. 13, 'The Shortness of Life and the Uncertainty of Riches', *Poems*, Vol. II, p. 452.

in the same year? 'As the lark ascends from its low bed on fluttering wing, and salutes the morning skies; so Mr Wordsworth's unpretending Muse, in russet guise, scales the summits of reflexion, while it makes the round earth its footstool and its home.'W[110] After these poetic flights, let me also, like the lark, return home to my subject . . . [Field here quotes from Milton's Preface. He remarks that the passage probably refers to the introduction of Sin and Death as allegorical persons in *Paradise Lost* and quotes Addison's objection: 'I cannot think that persons of such chimerical existence are proper actors in an epic poem; because there is not that measure of probability annexed to them, which is requisite in writings of this kind . . .']

CHAPTER VI   In poetry these personifications are not so necessary, since the Chorus of the Poet himself is always present, to explain and moralize everything; but Painting oftentimes cannot tell its story without such accessories; and, in my opinion, should be indulged with greater latitude. Nearly thirty years ago, I incurred the ridicule of a witty *coterie*, for defending the introduction of Cupid in Opie's picture of the Love-Sick Maid; and I remember that even Mr Haydon, who was present, said he did not think that, in this instance, the mind was sufficiently prepared for that introduction by any poetic tone in the painting. This was perhaps a very judicious and artistical observation. The Athenæus of that delightful young society, in his Notices to Correspondents, in the next number of a Magazine which he edited, pretended that I had sent him a paper 'On the powers of the pictorial Art', and regretted that I had left it in such an unfinished state. 'Having observed the feebleness ⟨he added⟩ of modern artists in the expression of the passions, and, with that refined taste which distinguishes him, despising the succedaneum of *This is a Bull*, he proposes, that when a young lady in love is to be described on canvas, the painter should mark the passion by the introduction of a little boy without breeches, shooting an arrow at her; in the delineation of an old lady in a rage, he recommends such auxiliaries as a griffin looking over her shoulders, or a tiger's head peeping out of her pocket-hole.'[111] I have since found, in Mr Opie's Lectures on painting, some remarks on the use of poetical

---

[110] **I never read that passage till I saw it here. Having little or no knowledge of H's writings except his first metaphysical Work—I had reasons for this which need not be named** [WW]. This is Wordsworth's last annotation to the *Memoirs*. He probably had read the passage however; cf. nn. 42, 48.

[111] Probably Leigh Hunt in the *Examiner*, c. 1811, but I have not found the piece. Not in the *Reflector*, recent collections of Hunt's essays, or mentioned in the *Autobiography*.

licence by a painter, which seem to be so decisive of the question, that they will not be out of place in this essay on the powers of poetry:—

'. . . His background, and every object in his composition, animate or inanimate, must all belong to one another and point to the same end; and under these restrictions, he tramples with impunity on all vulgar bounds, and scruples not, on great occasions, to press the elements into his service, or even to call in the aid of imaginary beings and supernatural agency. . . . I know of no one who has availed himself of poetic licence with more address than Sir Joshua Reynolds, in his celebrated picture of the death of Cardinal Beaufort . . . the visionary devil . . . clears up all ambiguity, by informing us that those are not bodily sufferings . . .[112] [if] nothing of a discordant nature [is] suffered to interpose, to check the progress of the imagination . . . poets and painters may do anything.'[113]

This proviso for consistency seems to be the great secret of historical painting and monumental sculpture; and this is doubtless what Mr Haydon meant by preparing the mind for allegorical accompaniments. But how could the mind be so poetically prepared in the two pictures in question, by Sir Joshua and Mr Opie, except by the natural elevation of the passions pourtrayed? Mr Haydon could not mean by stripping all the human actors in those pictures of their prose garments, as is too often done in statuary, and turning the hero out into the open air, naked, or in Roman costume. English historical and monumental art must preserve European dresses, however unpicturesque, reconciling the natural with the supernatural as well as it can; and here, as Mr Opie says, lies the mighty labour. Now it is that we see the vast superiority of poetry and romance over painting and sculpture. The penman finds no difficulty at all: it is he alone that can 'do anything', except what is technically called *portrait-painting*.

'Artists ⟨says Charles Lamb⟩ err in the confounding of poetical with pictorial subjects. In the latter, the exterior accidents are nearly everything; the unseen qualities as nothing. Othello's colour, the infirmities and corpulence of a Sir John Falstaff, do they haunt us perpetually in the reading? or are they obtruded on our conceptions,

---

[112] A note added later by Field to the Opie passage gives the entry for 15 July 1798 from Holcroft's *Diary*, 3 vols, London 1816, Vol. II, p. 276. This records an encounter between Burke and Reynolds in which the former argued that the 'absurd and ridiculous . . . blemish' of the devil should be obliterated.

[113] Field quotes lengthily from John Opie, *Lectures on Painting* . . ., London 1809, pp. 73-8, interrupting only to recall the Cupid of the *Love-Sick Maid*. Opie refers to *Macbeth*, *Lear* and *Paradise Lost* for literary examples of 'poetic licence'.

one time, for ninety-nine that we are lost in admiration at the respective moral or intellectual attributes of the character?'[114]

This is profoundly true, and applies too strongly to all the necessary embodyings of painting and sculpture. To spiritualize these too prominent carnalities is the triumph of the artist's genius. Did Corregio, in his exquisitely painted picture of Mercury instructing Cupid, feel that the flesh and blood of his Venus was too real, as it is, and so put wings at her back, for which there is no classical authority? The poet meets his hearers in the very element of ideality: it is the only medium of communication between the two parties. The artist has to convey the ideal by the material: the poet can only communicate the material by the ideal.

['Language ⟨says Shelley, in his Defence of Poetry⟩ is arbitrarily produced by the imagination, and has relation to thoughts alone; but all other materials, instruments and conditions of art have relations among each other . . . the intrinsic powers of the great masters of these arts may yield in no degree to that of those who have employed language as the hieroglyphic of their thoughts, has never equalled that of poets' . . .[115]]

I have now, after the lapse of a quarter of a century, written my paper 'On the powers of the pictorial Art'; and shall be happy to receive my old acquaintance's Answer to it, in another five and twenty years.

And yet sometimes the poet may gracefully work with no more than the painter's tools; as in the following pastoral picture by Mr Wordsworth, which I should like to see transferred to canvas by some poetical painter: I cannot think that it would be inconsistent or ridiculous:—

> Not so that pair whose youthful spirits dance . . .
>   The struggle, clap their wings for victory!
> ['The Stepping Stones', *River Duddon*, sonnet X, III, 250]
>
> Hoc ut dixit, Amor, sinistram ut aute,
> Dextram sternuit approbationem.
>   Catullus . . .[116]

[114] 'The Productions of Modern Art', *Works*, Vol. II, p. 264.
[115] Following the Shelley passage Field briefly debates some remarks on allegory in Allan Cunningham's *Lives of the . . . British Painters*, 6 vols, London 1829-33, Vol. I, p. 309.
[116] Field has inserted here an example of 'a poetical heresy, which may be called the converse of the doctrine that painting is mute poetry, namely that poetry should be vocal picture'. He quotes *Windsor Forest* l. 341, 'The Kennet swift, for silver eels renown'd' (*Poetical Works*, p. 47) and the comments of Darwin and Warton, referring to Montgomery's *Lectures on Poetry*, London 1833, as his source.

To return to our four great expositions of poetry,—in our own times, these elevated ideas have been still further developed by one, whom I am disposed to consider as the next great English poet to Milton, after Chaucer, Spenser and Shakspeare, namely Wordsworth, in the following passage from the Preface to his Lyrical Ballads:—

'Aristotle, I have been told, has said that poetry is the most philo-sophical of all writing. It is so; its object is truth, not individual and local, but general and operative . . . Except this one restriction, there is no object standing between the poet and the image of things; between this and the biographer and the historian, there are a thousand.' [II, 394-5]

Poetry is the most powerful, as well as the most philosophical, of all the fine arts. It can paint beyond Raffaelle. It is musical as is Apollo's lute; and it is, besides, reason, imagination, fancy, wit—not confined to one point of time, or to one place, but all these in endless pro-gression. Painting and sculpture are the most limited of all the fine arts. One moment is all they can seize; and the more poetic part of the imaginative is beyond their province. They require a certain actuality and tangibility. The only advantage, which they possess over their more ideal sisters, is that they ask no interpreter: they speak for themselves, and yet are dumb: they have been justly called the 'serenely silent arts'.[117]

> sedet, eternumque sedebit,
> Infelix Theseus.
>
> —Virgil . . .[118]

Music requires a skilful choir to command to any utterance of harmony; and even poetry a voice (the more skilful the better) to set the imprisoned speakers free. Till then, these arts are locked up, as it were, in cypher, and are lost without their key, as well as their voice.

> [But poets are confin'd in narrower space,
> To speak the language of their native place.
> The painter widely stretches his command;
> The pencil writes the tongue of ev'ry land.[119]]

Painting and sculpture speak all languages; and need only to be looked at. There they stand!

[117] Campbell [BF].
[118] Field here quotes also ll. 15-20, 'Ode on a Grecian Urn', *Poetical Works*, p. 261, and Wordsworth's sonnet 'Upon the Sight of a Beautiful Picture', Vol. III, p. 6.
[119] 'To Sir Godfrey Kneller', ll. 124-7, *Poems of John Dryden*, ed. James Kinsley, 4 vols, Oxford 1958, Vol. II, p. 861.

But in them Nature's copy's not eterne.[120]

The substance of painting fades with time; and even marble and brass perish with exposure to the atmosphere. The engraver preserves a faint reflection of the works of the painter and the sculptor, which, by succession from one burin [engraving tool] to another, may probably be continued for ever. The poet

> Exegit monumentum ære perennius,
> Regalique situ pyramidum altius;
> Quod non imber edax, non Aquilo impotens
> Possit diruere, aut innumerabilis
> Annorum series, et fuga temporum.
>
> Horatius.

Words, when a language is fixed, are the only things that of themselves last for ever, and are always as good as ever; for what Time takes away in living allusion and association, he adds in mysterious sanctity.

> [Where, Immortality! where can'st thou found
> Thy throne unperishing, but in the Song
> Of the true Bard, whose breath encrusts his theme
> Like to a petrifaction, which the stream
> Of Time will only make more durable?[121]]

I shall conclude this comparison with a passage from Burke's Inquiry into the Sublime and Beautiful:—

'Poetry and rhetoric do not succeed in exact description so well as painting does; their business is to affect, rather by sympathy, than imitation; to display rather the effect of things on the mind of the speaker or of others, than to present a clear idea of the things themselves. This is their most extensive province, and that in which they succeed the best. ... If the affectation be well conveyed, it will work its effect without any clear idea, often without any ideas at all, of the thing which has originally given rise to it.'[122]

The reader is here reminded of the quotation we made in our 4th Chapter, on the subject of *the vague*.[123]

And now let me add a few sentences on the subject of the third

---

[120] *Macbeth*, III. ii. 38. Field must surely have forgotten the context.
[121] 'Sicilian Arethusa', Horace Smith, *Poetical Works*, 2 vols, London 1846, Vol. I, p. 23.
[122] Field quotes from Pt. V, Sect. v, last para., and most of Sect. vii; *Works*, 12 vols, London 1837, Vol. I, pp. 257, 258-61. The sentences retained give the gist of the argument.
[123] See n. 88.

sister art, Music, whose written notes, equally with the words of Poetry, ought to last for ever [—her traditional modes, which sang in early Greece the worship of Jupiter and Apollo, are perhaps still preserved in our Gregorian and Ambrosean chaunts—] and whose effects upon the mind are in a much greater degree indebted to the vague ... [Field here has some confused remarks and quotations, partly added later, about the three arts. His main points are that music has the closer affinity with poetry, music and painting are more 'sensuous' than poetry, and painting has the single advantage of needing neither interpreter nor translator, but finally, 'There is nothing that words cannot tell'.]

CHAPTER VII To the mathematician, poetry is nonsense: its premises are false: what can it prove?

> Mount slowly, Sun, that we may journey long,
> By this dark hill protected from thy beams!
>
> [Bk II, ll. 111-12, V, 45]

exclaims Mr Wordsworth, in his Excursion. As if (the man of science would say) the course of the spheres could be retarded or quickened by any prayer of man!

> Between those heights,
> And on the top of either pinnacle,
> More keenly than elsewhere, in night's blue vault,
> Sparkle the stars, as of their station proud,
>
> [Bk II, ll. 719-23, V, 67]

sings another passage of the same poem. As if the stars had feelings and were conscious of a station that existed only to the eyes of the inhabitants of one little valley, in one small planet! says the astronomer. Such nonsense is nevertheless true poetry. 'The appropriate business of poetry ⟨says Mr Wordsworth⟩, which nevertheless, if genuine is as permanent as pure science, her appropriate employment, her privilege and her duty, is to treat of things not as they are, but as they appear—not as they exist in themselves, but as they seem to exist to the sense and to the passions.' [Essay Supplementary, II, 410]

> The poets, in their elegies and songs,
> Lamenting the departed, call the groves,
> They call upon the hills and streams to mourn,
> And senseless rocks; nor idly; for they speak

In these their invocations with a voice
Obedient to the strong creative power
Of human passion.

[*The Excursion*, Bk I, ll. 475-81, V, 24]

And mortal hopes, departed and o'erthrown,
Are mourn'd by man, and not by man alone ...
A constant interchange of growth and blight.

['Laodamia', ll. 165-74, II, 272]

At the same time, this privilege may be abused. Mr Wordsworth points out an instance of this abuse in the following lines of Cowper:

But the sound of the church-going bell
These vallies and rocks never heard;
Ne'er sigh'd at the sound of a knell,
Or smil'd when a sabbath appear'd.[124]

'These [last] two lines ⟨says he⟩ are in my opinion an instance of the language of passion, wrested from its proper use, and, from the mere circumstance of the composition being in metre, applied upon an occasion that does not justify such violent expressions.' [Appendix to 1802 Preface, II, 408] ...[125]

The poets often feign the rivers to stop their course, and other inanimate parts of nature, to hear the songs of Orpheus and the like. Virg. Ecl. viij. 4, vi. 85. But this is *dignus vindice nodus*. And herein consists the distinction. When some hero of the Iliad tells us that δορυ μαίνεται, his lance rages with eagerness to destroy, it is certainly too strong a personification for the occasion, and reminds us of the couplet in Martinus Scriblerus, quoted from Blackmore's Prince Arthur:

[124] 'Verses ... Alexander Selkirk', ll. 29-32, *Poetical Works*, pp. 311-2. Against 'church-going', which Wordsworth calls a 'strange abuse', Field notes, 'Mr Wordsworth cavils at this epithet, but surely it is as allowable as Shakspeare's "wry-neck'd fife" [*Mer. Ven.*, II. v. 30]'.

[125] Here Field has inserted a passage from *The Task*, I, 377-84, *Poetical Works*, p. 137, asking what Wordsworth would say to it and commenting vaguely, 'Even Oaks must not be ill-timed in their animation'. The text goes on with ll. 21-2 of Milton's third Latin elegy and Warton's comment (from Todd's Milton, VI, 190), 'Here is a beautiful picturesque image, but where the justness of the poetry is marred by the admission of a licentious fiction ... The conceit is that an oak should wonder at this'.

The mighty Stuffa threw a massy spear,
Which, with its errand pleas'd, sung thro' the air.[126]

When Lady Macbeth imprecates darkness to cover her,

That her keen knife see not the wound it makes,

it is perhaps too strong. But just and worthy is the terror of the soldiers commanded by Caesar to hew down the sacred grove, who dreaded (says Lucan) lest the axe aimed at the oak should fly back upon the striker:

si robora sacra ferirent,
In sua credebant rediturus membra secures.

And so Mr Wordsworth speaking of

that art
Divine of words, quickening insensate things.
From the submissive necks of guiltless men
Stretch'd on the block, the glittering axe recoils.

['Why, Minstrel . . .', ll. 7-10, III, 6-7] . . .[127]

But the most forcible illustration of this doctrine is to be found in the following two passages, the former by Lord Chesterfield being a mere conceit or *jeu d'esprit*:

The dews of the evening most carefully shun:
Those tears of the sky for the loss of the sun.

The latter is from the Paradise Lost, and is justly in deep earnest. 'After the transgression of Adam ⟨continues Mr Wordsworth⟩ Milton, with other appearances of sympathising Nature, thus marks the immediate consequence:

Sky lowered, and muttering thunder some sad drops
Wept as completion of the mortal sin.

---

[126] *The Art of Sinking in Poetry*, ed. E. L. Stevens, New York 1952, p. 55. The examples from the *Iliad* and from *Macbeth* and Lucan (below) are in Johnson's *Rambler* No. 168 (*Works*, Yale edn, Vol. V, pp. 127-8). But see Field's argument against Johnson's account of *Macbeth*, I. v. 48-52 here, summarised in n. 180 below; this may suggest that he is citing common examples rather than simply borrowing without acknowledgement.

[127] Here Field has inserted four further examples: Collins, 'Ode to Liberty', l. 12, *Poetical Works of Gray and Collins*, ed. A. L. Poole, Oxford 1937, p. 261; 'Song at the Feast of Brougham Castle', ll. 142-9, II, 258; *1HIV*, I. iii. 101-06; *RIII*, IV. i. 97-103. He approves of the second and fourth, rejecting the comment of 'unimaginative Johnson' that 'To call the Tower nurse and playfellow is very harsh' (*Works*, Vol. VIII, p. 625).

The associating link is the same in each instance. Dew or rain, not distinguishable from the liquid substance of tears, are employed as indications of sorrow. A flash of surprise is the effect in the former case, a flash of surprise and nothing more; for the nature of things does not sustain the imagination. In the latter, the effects from the act of which there is this immediate consequence and visible sign are so momentous, that the mind acknowledges the justice and reasonableness of the sympathy in Nature so manifested; and the sky weeps drops of water, as if with human eyes, as "Earth had before trembled from her entrails, and Nature given a second groan".'[128]

So when Dido, in the fourth Aeneid, yielded to that fatal temptation, which ruined her, Virgil tells us that the earth trembled, the heavens were filled with flashes of lightning, and the nymphs howled upon the mountain-tops.[129]

But it is enough that these sympathies of Nature appear to the Poet, and (if the poet so pleases) to the immediate subjects of his poetry. The rest of his *dramatis personae* are no more bound to notice them than the rest of the world. Dr Greenwood, in his notes on Milton, says:— '. . . I wonder that this accurate and careful writer hath not hinted something at Adam's thoughts upon the first convulsion, when he was in a state of innocence calmness and retirement. As "Nature thro' all her works gave signs of woe", he could not but be very sensible of it; and if so, he must certainly be startled at a phenomenon so strange and new. This, I think, deserved in some measure to be accounted for . . .' [But] the poet knew best.

> Adam the whiles
> Waiting, desirous, her return, had wove
> Of choicest flowers a garland, to adorn
> Her tresses, and her rural labours crown,
> As reapers oft are wont their harvest-queen.[130]

Does not this afford a more beautiful contrast and repose, after the awfulness of the 'first disobedience'? 'Andromache ⟨says Bishop Newton⟩ is thus described as amusing herself and preparing for the return of Hector, not knowing that he was already slain by Achilles. Iliad xxij, 440.'

[128] 1815 Preface, II, 442. Both illustrations, from Chesterfield's 'Advice to a Lady in Autumn' and *Paradise Lost* IX, 1,002-03, are of course Wordsworth's To the first, Field notes 'But as the earth doth weep, the sun being set' (*Lucrece* l. 1,216).

[129] Here Field has inserted the lines, *Aeneid*, IV, 166-8, followed by a passage which 'everybody must feel . . . is mere false gallop', *The Troublesome Reign of King John*, ed. F. J. Furnivall and J. Monro, London 1913, Vol. I, pp. 255-64

[130] *Paradise Lost*, IX, 818-42; notes from Todd's edition.

An excellent critic in the Quarterly Review for November 1834 (perhaps Mr Henry Taylor) is of opinion that Mr Wordsworth himself has gone too far in this poetical licence, and cites the following as instances: ['Immortality Ode', ll. 12-13, 198-9, IV, 279, 285; *The Excursion*, Bk I, ll. 201-03, V, 15.] It was hardly fair in the critic to isolate these passages. Much depends upon the state of feeling, to which the previous music had elevated the poet. The following is perhaps a bolder instance; but mark how the artist prepares his hearer even by the rhyme for the climax word:—

> With heart as calm as lakes that sleep
>   In frosty moonlight glistening:
> Or mountain-rivers, where they creep
>   Along a channel smooth and deep,
> To their own far-off murmurs listening.
>
> ['Memory', ll. 25-30, IV, 101-2]

[I consider Mr Wordsworth's use of this poetic licence to be quite modest compared with the liberties which had been accustomed without any preparation to be taken by Ovid and Cowley, and their Roman and English imitators. Exempli gratia . . .[31] In such poetry as this, the writer's only object is to shew his wit. There is no such belief or truth pretended, as exists in all Mr Wordsworth's effusions.] The reviewer should have recollected that it is Mr Wordsworth's poetic faith,

> That a rich loving-kindness, redundantly kind,
> Moves all nature to gladness and mirth;
>   The showers of the Spring
>   Rouse the birds and they sing,
> If the wind do but stir for *his* proper delight,
> Each leaf, that and this, his neighbour will kiss,
> Each wave, one and t'other speeds after *his* brother;
> They are happy for that is their right.
>
> ['Stray Pleasures', ll. 29-36, II, 160-1]

What does the reviewer say to the boldness of these personifications? They can only be excused in an enthusiast. They are true in that aspect of Nature long looked at; and to that mood of mind, deeply meditated.

The ordinary trope in question is constantly and systematically abused by Mr Shelley. For instance, in his tragedy of the Cenci, in a mere narrative passage, without any particular sympathy with the

[31] The examples are, 'ambiguo lapsu, refluitque, fluitque, Occurrensque sibi venturas aspicit medas', Ovid; and Spratt's 'On his Mistress Drown'd'.

subject, on the part of the interlocutrix, the poet makes her pump passion
as follows ...[132] How timid was Gray in the use of these figures!
His friend Richard West has a line in his Ode on the approach of May:

> Each budding flow'ret calls for thee.

Even without the preparation of the poem, one would have thought
this might have been allowed. But no: Mr Gray says:— 'The exclama-
tion of the flowers is a little step too far'. In his youth, Gray had
committed the following enormity, in a translation from Statius
describing a prize disc-player:

> The orb on high, tenacious of its course,
> True to the mighty arm that gave it force,
> Far overleaps all bound, and *joys to see*
> Its antient lord secure of victory.[133]

But in his chaster years, when Mr Gray requires sympathy, he takes
no liberties with Nature, but calls upon his lawful Muse, and begets
the personified passions, male and female begetteth he them,—printer-
made poetry, in which (as Mr Coleridge says) 'it depends wholly on
the compositor's putting, or not putting, a capital letter, whether the
words shall be personifications or mere abstractions'[134]—'a personated
virtue or vice ⟨to repeat the words of the Preface to the Theatrum
Poetarum⟩ rising out of the ground and uttering a speech'. These
fanciful creations should be very sparingly introduced ...[135]

Can anything be more tiresome than such a glut of abstractions or
personifications as the following, from Gray's Ode on the Pleasures of
Vicissitude? ...[136] Collins was also too fond of this trick, and it
became the regular miscellany and magazine Ode-manufacture, down
to Mr Wordsworth's time. Take an example of this style of poetry
from so respectable a writer as Dr Langhorne, in his Hymn to Humanity
...[137] Sir Egerton Brydges, in his preference of Collins to Gray, in

---

[132] III, i, 243-55, *Poetical Works*, ed. T. Hutchinson, Oxford 1934, p. 302. Field
has underlined, 'a mighty rock ... Sustained itself, *with terror and with toil*,
... *the agony With which it clings*'.

[133] See *Corr.*, Vol. I, pp. 42, 201-2, and *Poems*, ed. H. W. Starr and J. R.
Hendrickson, Oxford 1966, p. 56.

[134] Cf. *Table Talk*, Oxford 1917, pp. 318-19.

[135] Field here quotes from *Spectator* No. 357, 'I do not know any imaginary
person ... richness of his imagination', Bond, Vol. III, pp. 338-9.

[136] ll. 33-6, 41-4, *Poems*, pp. 101-2.

[137] Field here quotes ll. 6-21 (*Chalmer's English Poets*, Vol. XVI, p. 467), with the
comment between the stanzas, 'Sorrow and Grief are here as in Gray two
persons. Here the words have all capital letters, and are therefore personifications. In the next stanza, the words *joy* and *woe* are without capitals, and are
therefore mere abstractions; and Sorrow, instead of living in a cell, gets into

which I agree with him, attempts to distinguish the personifications of the two poets by saying that those of Gray are human beings invested with some of the attributes of angels, while those of Collins are pure angels. The personifications are all of human passions or emotions, virtues or vices, and should relish of humanity to be interesting to man. But I do not perceive the difference, which Sir Egerton would point out [and should be very sorry if I could. Pure angels would be some such personifications as that in the Oxford copy of verses on the two Suttons, commencing

> Inoculation! heavenly maid! descend![138]

or like the Spaniards, who, in their confusion of reality with truth, have personified the Immaculate Conception.] All I can see is, that they are introduced less poetically and sublimely by Gray than by Collins.

The poet is the most selfish egotist in the world. It is the duty of his art to refer everything to himself, and his own feelings. All nature must sympathise with him and the moods of his little hour. Should he be pleased to pipe, the hills must dance: should it be his humour to mourn, the skies must weep.

> Sun, moon and stars, all struggle in the toils
> Of mortal sympathy.
>
> ['Why, Minstrel ...', ll. 11-13, III, 7]

The poet throws himself into all things—makes his present passion the centre of all nature—and it is the triumph of his art to compel his reader to feel that all this is probable and natural—imaginative but still reasonable—not nonsense, but highest sense and truth—and, above all, delightful ...[139] He must not impudently exclaim—

> Thus have I seen, in Araby the blest,
> A phoenix couch'd upon her funeral nest.[140]

---

man's eye'. After this he has inserted a line from Collins, 'Rage grasps the sword, while Pity melts the eyes' ('Epistle to Sir Thomas Hanmer', l. 144, *Poetical Works of Gray and Collins*, p. 321), asking if it is less ludicrous than 'The father softens, but the Governor's resolv'd', from Sheridan's *Critic*.

[138] Field has probably borrowed the example from *Biog. Lit.*, Vol. II, p. 66.

[139] Field here quotes ten lines from 'Frost at Midnight', 1812 *Poetical Register* text ('Haply hence, ... not uninvited'), *Poems*, Vol. I, p. 241; and *Paradise Lost*, II, 533-41, with Cowper's comment on l. 533, 'A captious critic might object to this simile. ... It is always lawful for a poet ... to realize a creature of the fancy, merely for the sake of embellishment and illustration' (*Commentary on Paradise Lost, Works*, ed. R. Southey, 15 vols, London 1835-7, Vol. XV, p. 320).

[140] *The Art of Sinking in Poetry*, p. 22.

But he is not to be proscribed from all allusion to the phoenix, 'which ⟨says Dr Johnson, carping at Milton⟩[141] is so evidently contrary to reason and nature, that it ought never to be mentioned but as a fable, in any serious poem'. Aristotle says, the poet may represent things such as they are, or such as they should be, or such *as they are believed to be*. And so Dryden, in one of his spirited prefaces:— 'For my part, I am of opinion that neither Homer, Virgil, Statius, Ariosto, Tasso, nor our English Spenser, could have formed their poems half so beautiful, without these gods and spirits. ... It is enough that in all ages and religions, the greater part of mankind have believed the power of magic, and that there are spirits and spectres which have appeared. This (I say) is foundation enough for poetry'.[142]

Dr Rees, in the article Poetry, in his Cyclopaedia, denies this; and says that 'as nothing unnatural can please, poetry ... ought as nearly as possible to conform to nature'.[143] But it is not true that nothing

---

[141] See the criticisms on Milton in the Rambler, and the character of 'Minim the critic' in the Idler [No. 61], in which the following passage occurs:— 'From blank verse he makes an easy transition to Milton, whom he produces as an example of the slow advance of lasting reputation. ... The lines that are commonly thought rugged and unmusical, he conceives to have been written to temper the melodious luxury of the rest, or to express things by a proper cadence; for he scarcely finds a verse that has not this favorite beauty' [*Works*, Yale edn, Vol. II, p. 191, ed. W. J. Bate, John Bullitt, L. F. Powell, 1963]. Dr Johnson meant this for banter. I can only say that if these be crotchets, my name is Minim. The lines that Dr Johnson thought rugged and unmusical I conceive to have been written to temper the melodious luxury of the rest, or to express things by a proper cadence; for I scarcely find a verse that has not this favorite beauty. This then was the idea of a false critic in Dr Johnson's time. It is singular that Mr Hazlitt, in our days, without adverting to this paper, has portrayed the character of a 'common-place critic' in a series of essays called The Round Table, which, with all its paradoxes, is at least as entertaining as the Idler:— 'He ⟨the commonplace critic⟩ thinks Milton's pedantry a great blemish in his writings, and that Paradise Lost has many prosaic passages in it. He considers Dr Johnson as a great critic' [*Works*, IV, 38]. Now, in its turn, it is Dr Johnson's opinion that is the common-place, and Mr Minim's judgment is affirmed. So it will be or rather is with Mr Jeffrey's poetical sentences. Dr Johnson's standard here is 'what is commonly thought', and Mr Jeffrey erects 'the judgment of the public' as what the poet ought to follow, not to lead. [Here the relevant passage from 'Edinb. Rev. vol. xvij p. 430' has been del.] It would be just the same nowadays with a new Paradise Lost. It would be censured by a Johnson or a Jeffrey as not what is commonly thought poetry by the judgment of the public, and neglected by that public accordingly, till Time should give influence and credit to the taste of the judicious few [BF]. Johnson's 'carping' was at *Paradise Lost*, V, 272.

[142] 'An Essay of Heroic Plays', *Essays of John Dryden*, ed. W. P. Ker, 2 vols, Oxford 1900, Vol. I, pp. 152-3.

[143] Abraham Rees, ed., *The New Cyclopaedia, or Universal Dictionary* ..., 45 vols, London 1802-20.

unnatural can please. Our imagination creates another and a higher nature than the *rerum natura*, 'something preternatural 〈as Warton says〉 and consequently false, but therefore more poetical', and consequently more pleasing. Dr Johnson reprobates the 'long narration', as he styles it, about Sabrina, in Comus, which he says 'is of no use because it is *false*, and therefore unsuitable to a *good* being.' 'By the poetical reader 〈answers Mr Warton〉 this fiction is considered as true. . . . Something. . . more poetical, was necessary for the present distress.'[144]

And so Bishop Hurd, in his excellent remarks on the Faëry Queen, says:— 'The source of bad criticism, as universally of bad philosophy, is the abuse of terms. A poet, they say, must follow nature; and by nature, we are to suppose, can only be meant the known and experienced course of affairs in this world. . . . [But] in the poet's world all is marvellous and extraordinary, yet not *unnatural* in one sense, as it agrees to the conceptions, that are readily entertained of these magical and wonder-working natures'.[145]

'When gross errors in philosophy 〈continues Dr Rees, by which he means Science, which he confounds with the philosophy of poetry〉 . . . are introduced into the works of the poet . . . they tend to obstruct one of the principal aims of poetry, and not only to diminish its utility, but to render it instrumental in supporting and disseminating fallacious opinions.' And then the learned doctor quotes the passage from Milton [*Paradise Lost*, VII, 370-9] which ascribes to the sun male, and to the moon female, light. As if any one read Homer, Virgil or Milton for their science! It is not 'one of the principal aims of poetry' to teach physics. The fault of that passage is not its false science, but the pedantry of introducing the distinction at all. It was not necessary for the archangel Raphael, however affable, to be so minute in describing to Adam the great system of the universe. He should have imitated the wise vagueness of the holy Scriptures, which were never meant to teach us geology, or astronomy, and which are no more censurable than the Poet, for accommodating their incidental science to the opinions of the times.

> This to attain, whether Heaven move or Earth,
> Imports not, if thou reckon right; the rest
> From man or angel, the Great Architect
> Did wisely to conceal, and not divulge
> His secrets, to be scann'd by them who ought
> Rather admire.

[144] See notes to *Comus*, l. 821, in Todd's Milton, Vol. V, p. 382.
[145] *Hurd's Letters on Chivalry and Romance*, ed. E. J. Morley, London 1911, p. 138.

Bishop Newton, in commenting upon a similar passage of this great Bard, shows a better sense of poetry, by merely 'wishing that the author had taken more care what notions of philosophy he had put into the mouth of an archangel. . . . But if he had written after the late discoveries and improvements in science, he would have written in another manner'.[146]

'The harmony of the spheres ⟨continues Dr Rees⟩, first taught by the Pythagoreans, is so pleasing to the imagination, that it is not surprising, that the poets should have adopted it; and Milton has given such a view of it, as wants nothing but philosophical truth, to render it delightful [*Paradise Lost*, V, 620-7] . . .' Instead of *philosophical* truth, Dr Rees, as well as Bishop Newton, should have said *scientific* truth. This passage does possess the most philosophical truth—'truth ⟨as Mr Wordsworth says⟩ not standing upon external testimony, but carried alive into the heart by passion' [Preface, II, 394-5]—by poetry.

> Truths of the heart flock in with eager pace,
> And Fancy greets them with a fond embrace.
>
> ['The Warning', ll. 24-5, IV, 110]

And I appeal to everyone who has a heart, whether scientific truth, sublime as the facts of astronomy are, would not have frozen all that is delightful out of this poetical view of the harmony of the spheres . . . [Field here quotes Akenside's lines on the intenser pleasure given by the scientific explanation of the rainbow and his attempt to versify it, commenting 'It appears to me to be unintelligible science and bad poetry'. He thinks 'the rainbow's hues shine a little more pleasing' in Coleridge's lines,

> As tho' the spirits of all lovely flowers,
> Inweaving each its wreath, and dewy crown,
> Or ere they sank to earth in vernal showers,
> Had built a bridge to tempt the angels down.

These lead him to quote four stanzas from Campbell's 'To the Rainbow', including the lines 'I ask not proud Philosophy To teach me what thou art. . . . What lovely visions yield their place To cold material laws!', and then Keats's famous lines from 'Lamia', 'Do not all charms fly At the mere touch of cold philosophy? . . . Unweave a rainbow', with the comment, 'And this is true in many cases'.[147] But

---

146 *Paradise Lost*, VIII, 70-75; and part of Newton's n. to V, 415-20, from Todd's Milton, Vol. II, p. 409.
147 *Pleasures of Imagination* (1744), II, *Poetical Works of Akenside and Dyer*, ed. R. A. Willmott, London 1855, p. 24; 'The Two Founts', ll. 21-4, *Poems*, Vol. I, p. 454; 'To the Rainbow', st. 1-4, *Poetical Works*, ed. J. L. Robertson, Oxford 1907, p. 233; 'Lamia', ll. 229-37, *Poetical Works*, p. 212.

to the Poet, Science brings, in return, visions of her own. Optics have their own poetry. Poetry must not pretend to be scientific, as Dr Akenside or Dr Darwin would have made her; but Science has its poetical aspect. Poetry is not useful knowledge for its own sake, or for the mere advancement of civilized society. It is (as Mr Wordsworth says) 'the breath and finer spirit of all knowledge . . . If the time should ever come when what is now called Science, thus familiarized to men, shall be ready to put on, as it were, a form of flesh and blood, the Poet will lend his divine spirit to the transfiguration, and will welcome the Being thus produced, as a dear and genuine inmate of the household of Man' [Preface, II, 396-7].[148]

> Desire we past illusions to recall?
> To re-instate wild Fancy, would we hide
> Truths, whose thick veil Science has drawn aside? . . .
> Imaginative Faith! can'st overleap,
> In progress toward the fount of Love.
>
> [*Itinerary Poems XIV*, ll. 1-11, IV, 31-2]

CHAPTER VIII   What I view as the restoration of natural and legitimate poetry, after the long and dazzling usurpation of Dryden and Pope, was made in the year 1798, by the publication of the Lyrical Ballads of Messrs Wordsworth and Coleridge.

'They were published ⟨says Mr Wordsworth⟩ as an experiment which I hoped might be of some use, to ascertain how far, by fitting to metrical arrangement a selection of the real language of men, in a state of vivid sensation, that sort of pleasure, and that quantity of pleasure, may be imparted, which a poet may rationally endeavour to impart . . .' [II, 384, 386-7][149]

Mr Wordsworth might have quoted Aristotle again here: 'The diction ⟨he says⟩ should be most laboured in the idle parts of the poem—those in which neither manners nor sentiment prevail, for the manners and sentiments are only obscured by too splendid a diction'.

[148] Field omits, 'Emphatically may it be said . . . thoughts are everywhere' and 'Poetry is the first and last of all knowledge—it is as immortal as the heart of man'.
[149] Field follows the second sentence of the Preface with the passage 'The principal objects . . . fickle appetites of their own creation', adding Wordsworth's fn. on Chaucer. He interrupts to remark on the similarity to Burke 'in a passage before quoted' (in Ch. VI) and to Sir Walter Scott's comment in the Preface to *The Antiquary* that in that novel and in *Guy Mannering* he had sought his principal personages and some scenes in the 'lower orders' because they 'are less restrained by the habit of suppressing their feelings, and because I agree with Mr Wordsworth that they seldom fail to express them in the strongest and most powerful language'.

And so in his 'Rhetoric' . . . he observes that such a degree of embellishment, as forces on the hearer the idea of labour and art and preparation,
is to be avoided . . . 'The best way to conceal artifice, and make your
language appear easy and natural, is by forming it chiefly of the words
and phrases of customary speech, properly selected, as Euripides does,
who first set the example'.[150]

And so Sir William D'Avenant, in the Preface before quoted
[Chapter VI] . . . The secret is, as Roger Ascham says, to think like the
wise, but to speak like the common people. So too says Dryden,
which shews that Mr Wordsworth's theory, as it is called, is nothing
more than a return to nature:— 'As for the turn of words . . . in strong
passion [they are] always to be shunned, because passions are serious
and will admit no playing . . . Chaucer writ with more simplicity, and
followed nature more closely, than to use them'.[151]

Dr Johnson, like Pope in other fine arts, had occasional glimpses of
this truth in poetry—as where he says in his Preface to Shakspeare:—
'Shakspeare has no heroes: his scenes are occupied only by men, who
act and speak as the reader thinks he should himself have spoken or
acted on the same occasion . . . he has not only shown human nature,
as it acts in real exigencies, but as it would be found in trials to which
it cannot be exposed'. And in another place:— 'Addison speaks the
language of poets, and Shakspeare of men'.[152] And yet Addison, as a
critic himself, could feel the merit of simplicity, as he has amply shown
in his Critique on Chevy Chase, and the following pretty allegory
in the Guardian, No. 32 . . .[153]

[So Pope, in his bad and indecent Imitations of English poets, has the
profaneness to burlesque the Faëry Queen, and this so pleased Shenstone
that, whereas before he says he could not read Spenser, he was now led
to consider him ludicrously, and 'in that light ⟨he adds⟩ he could read
him with pleasure'. 'We owe the Schoolmistress ⟨says Mr P. Cunning-
ham⟩[154] to this ill-taste and this complete misconception of Spenser'.]
Shenstone actually meant it for burlesque, but Nature carried it
through, as she had before made earnest of Gay's Pastorals, which were

---

[150] Treatise on Poetry, p. iii, s. 6. Twining's Aristotle, p. 470 [BF].
[151] 'Preface to the Fables', *Essays of John Dryden*, Vol. II, p. 257.
[152] *Works*, Yale edn, Vol. VII, ed. A. Sherbo, New Haven and London 1968,
pp. 64-5, 84.
[153] 'Chevy Chase', *Spectator* Nos 70, 74, Bond, Vol. I, pp. 298-303, 315-22.
Guardian No. 32 was actually written by Steele; in it the descendants of
Amyntas and Amaryllis are Theocritus, Virgil, Spenser and Philips—but not
Pope. Field goes on to mention Pope's rejoinder to this slight to 'his own
puerile pastorals' in *Guardian* No. 40, that they were 'by no means pastorals,
but something better'.
[154] Campbell's Specimens of the Poets, p. 450 [BF].

written in conspiracy with Pope, in the spirit of his critique [*Guardian*
No. 40], and in ridicule of Philips; so much will Nature do even for
those who only seem to worship her. See the article entitled 'Shenstone's
Schoolmistress', in Mr D'Israeli's Curiosities of Literature, second series,
where the suppressed preface to the first edition of that poem may be
read, in which its author pretends to think Philips's 'Little charm of
placid mien' mere childishness (which it is not) and says that 'he has
added a ludicrous index to his *Schoolmistress* to show (fools) that he is
in jest'.[155] I will indulge my fun a little further upon the subject of
Shenstone, who, with all his faults, was the legitimate successor of
Philips: Shenstone had unintentionally discovered the true vein, and, if
he had had the courage to follow it whithersoever it led—to put implicit
faith in Nature, he might have anticipated the rural poetry of Wordsworth by more than half a century. The ballad of 'Jemmy Dawson'
leaves nothing, and the well-known Pastoral Ballad little, to be
desired. But the great secret of Shenstone's failure in all the rest of his
poetry, except the Schoolmistress, in the second edition of which he
took courage to throw off the grinning masque, is that he was afraid
to trust to Nature wholly:— it was only his vanity, that was in rural
scenes—his heart was far away—in towered cities, with Ambition and
Wealth. Shenstone, like Mr Wordsworth, writes a prefatory essay to
his Elegies, in which he says that, 'if he describes a rural landskip or
unfolds the train of sentiments it inspired, he fairly drew his picture
from the spot, and felt very sensibly the affection he communicates.
If he speaks of his humble shed, his flocks and his fleeces, *he* does not
counterfeit the scene, who having (whether from choice or necessity
is not material[156]) retired betimes to country solitudes, and sought his
happiness in rural employments, has a right to consider himself as a
real shepherd. The flocks, the meadows, and the grottoes, are his own,
and the embellishment of his farm his sole amusement. As the sentiments therefore were inspired by Nature, and that in the earlier part of
his life, he hopes they will retain a natural appearance, diffusing at
least some part of that amusement, which he freely acknowledges he
received from the composition of them'.[157] If all these facts were true,
there would be no need to *hope* the verses would retain a natural
appearance. They would be really natural, like Mr Wordsworth's; but
Shenstone was impairing his little fortune by *embellishing*, as he called
it, his grounds, and envying the rich their power to build a villa upon

---

[155] *Curiosities of Literature*, ed. I. D'Israeli, second series, 3 vols, London 1823,
Vol. I, pp. 245-53.
[156] Indeed but it is most material. Mr Wordsworth's retirement was emphatically
from choice [BF].
[157] *Works*, 2 vols, Edinburgh 1765, Vol. I, pp. 9-10.

them; instead of devoting himself to the disinterested love of the country. The consequence was that Nature betrayed the heart that really loved her not; and these Elegies, in spite of their vindication by Mr D'Israeli, are, for the most part, false fires. In the same series of 'Curiosities of Literature', we have a second article entitled 'Shenstone vindicated', from which I take the liberty of extracting the following passages, as novel illustrations of the life and poetry of Shenstone . . .[158]

To return to Pope,—is it not strange that he, who, in the arts of architecture and gardening, could see the beauty of simplicity so clearly as to pen the following paragraph, should be such an artificial poet? 'Arts ⟨says he⟩ are taken from nature; and, after a thousand vain efforts for improvements, are best when they return to their first simplicity.'[159] This is the whole of what is called Mr Wordsworth's theory. It is no novel discovery—no secret magic. [It was just the same with Roman literature. . . . If the empire had not fallen, Rome might have had its Wordsworth, some Valerius Dictus. In the days of Pope, Shakspeare was considered as little better than a barbarian. I confess, that I carry my love for simplicity so far as to prefer single flowers to double ones. I look upon Darwin and Moore as upon carnations and pickotees [*sic*: bunch of artificial flowers]. I do not like to see stamina converted by high manuring and artificial heat into petals.] Mr Wordsworth's return to nature may be further illustrated by the difference between the inspired hebraic poetry of the Bible, and all other oriental verse;[160] and he himself actually illustrates it by quoting

---

[158] *Curiosities of Literature*, Vol. II, pp. 62-4. Field comments sarcastically on the account of Shenstone's relations with Mary Cutler, e.g., 'whom he never married,—faithless to the last'.

[159] *Joseph Spence, Observations, Anecdotes and Characters*, ed. James M. Osborne, 2 vols, Oxford 1966, Vol. I, p. 236.

[160] Bishop Lowth, in his Lectures on the Poetry of the Hebrews [written in Latin], has not made this observation, and his translator Mr Gregory seems to prefer the paraphrases of English versifiers to the Scriptural originals, and thus proves that, whoever may be edified by that author, the translator was not. . . . it is to be wished that Mr Gregory had not newly translated into English every quotation from the Bible. The language of our old English version has now become sacred. . . . [it] was made at the purest epoch of our language, soon after Spenser and Shakspeare had fixed its simplicity for ever [BF]. The note continues, somewhat inconsequentially, with a comparison of Pope's line in his *Messiah*, 'He wipes the tears for ever from our eyes' (l. 46, *Poetical Works*, p. 34) with Steele's 'jingle' alteration, 'From every face he wipes off every tear' (see new 'Twickenham' *Pope*, Vol. I, London 1961, p. 100, for Steele's reasons), which, Field thinks, 'by directing the mind to individual faces, and what is worse to individual tears, produces a ludicrous effect', unlike 'the great original passage in Isaiah'. The note ends with a 'test of bad poetry' from 'Richard Duke, one of Dr Johnson's poets [*Lives*, Vol. II, pp. 24-5]': 'Whene'er you speak with what delight we hear, You call up every soul to every ear'.

the beautiful passage, 'Go to the Ant, thou Sluggard', &c. in contrast
with Dr Johnson's paraphrase of the same . . .[161]

After this, the following improvements in diction suggested by a
humorous writer in the Monthly Chronicle upon the 'And there was
light' and 'Thou art the man' of Scripture, are scarcely exaggerations:—

'And accordingly, in an incredibly short space of time, the luminous
principle diffused itself over all the objects of visible nature'.

'Why you are the very individual I have been all along alluding
to'.

I shall conclude these inculcations of Simplicity, with the last two
stanzas of Collins's Ode to that nymph . . .[162]

To proceed with Mr Wordsworth's Preface,—His views of 'humble
and rustic life' are the very converse of Mr Crabbe's, at least in theory.
It will be seen that both poets fell off, or rather rose, in practice.
Something must be allowed for the difference between the peasantry
of the Cumberland mountains, and that of Aldborough in Suffolk.
Mr Crabbe says that

> cast by Fortune on a frowning coast,
> Which neither groves nor happy vallies boast ⟨boasts⟩,
> Where other cares than those the Muse relates,
> And other shepherds, dwell, with other mates,
> By such examples taught I paint the cot
> As Truth will paint it, and as Bards will not.[163]

We have seen that it is the business of the higher order of poetry, in
the words of Bacon, not 'to buckle and bow the mind unto the nature
of things, but to submit the shows of things to the desires of the
mind'; but I have no objection to a Hogarthian picture. There is room

---

[161] Field here quotes the comparison in the Appendix (Vol. II, p. 407) of *The
Vanity of Human Wishes* with *Proverbs*, vi, 1-11. Later he added Croker's
account of Dr Johnson on Harwood's Liberal Translation of the New Testa-
ment: 'The passage which first caught his eye was from that sublime apostrophe
in St. John, upon the raising of Lazarus, "Jesus wept", which Harwood had
conceitedly rendered, "And Jesus, the Saviour of the world, burst into a
flood of tears". He contemptuously threw the book aside, exclaiming
"Puppy!"'. Field comments, 'If the Scriptures had been written in this style,
it would have impeached not only their taste, but their truth, of which one of
the strongest evidences is the absence of any attempt on the part of the sacred
writers to elevate—to magnify—to expatiate . . .'
[162] *Poetical Works of Gray and Collins*, pp. 252-3.
[163] *The Village*, Bk I, ll. 49-54, *Tales, 1812*, ed. H. Mills, Cambridge 1967,
p. 2.

for all schools, in the great gallery of poetry. . . .[164] But I cannot think that it is *truth* that paints Mr Crabbe's cottage. It may be, what D'Avenant calls, a selected diary of fortune, but it is not the general history of nature. It may be the particular fact, but it is not general truth. I think that the peasantry of all countries are generally happy and not miserable. It is surely a rare concatenation of misfortunes, that has combined in Mr Crabbe's 'Village' a parish apothecary who murders his pauper, and a priest who lets him be buried without a funeral service.[165] Mr Crabbe in the course of his eventful life filled both of these offices, but this is surely not a correct picture of them. He feels that poetry cannot go on in this strain, and accordingly in the next book of his poem, he admits that there are found amid the evils of a laborious life, some views of tranquillity and happiness, and proceeds to describe the repose and pleasure of a summer sabbath, like any other true poet, that 'derives his light from Heaven'; for he has an instinct that it is his business to delight in the main, and that his painful views of life can only be admitted by way of contrast. And next he finds that the higher classes have also their peculiar distresses; and tells the poet to

> Forbear to envy those you call the great,
> And know, amid the blessings they possess,
> They are, like you, the victims of distress.[166]

So that we are all to be unhappy together: And then he concludes the book with a panegyric on 'his grace ⟨as he calls him⟩ the Duke of Rutland'.

'There will also be found in these volumes ⟨Mr Wordsworth adds⟩ little of what is usually called poetic diction . . . the language of these lines does in no respect differ from that of good prose'. [II, 390-1][167]

[164] Field here quotes some lines from Drayton ('What is he alone That of himself can say He's heir of Helicon'); 'Anon' ('The nightingale doth never say, . . . Why sing you not so sweet as I? . . . These various notes are all but one'); and Wordsworth's lines now (from 1845) at the beginning of *Poetical Works*, I, 1, ll. 1-3, which he would have known from their earlier place among the Poems of Sentiment and Reflection.

[165] It is singular that this very passage [Bk I, ll. 274-346, *Tales*, pp. 7-9] should be quoted by Mr Jeffrey as 'manly sense and correct painting,' compared with what he calls the 'childish and absurd affectations' of Mr Wordsworth. See Edinb. Rev. vol. XII p. 137 [BF, added later].

[166] *The Village*, Bk II, ll. 102-41, *Tales*, p. 12.

[167] Field includes Gray's sonnet on Richard West but omits 'Without being culpably particular . . . if he wishes to be pleased with these volumes'. In notes he quotes Lowth's remark that 'the language of poetry differs very widely from that of all other kinds of composition', and Gray's that 'the language of the age is never the language of poetry', commenting that the latter is 'a doctrine of which even Mr Headley and Dr Warton approve. See Beauties of Antient English Poets, vol. i, p. XX 1787. Warton's Pope, vol. i p. 220, 1797.'

Here I cannot help thinking that Mr Wordsworth's right principles of poetry have carried his theory, though not his practice, a little too far. I can by no means assent to the last assertion. The language of the first three of the lines in question [Gray's sonnet on Richard West, ll. 6-8] is too inverted and metaphorical for prose. Let us take every line separately. One gentleman, writing a letter to another on the death of a friend, might perhaps be allowed by good taste to say, provided the former part of the epistle had prepared the mind for it,—'These eyes do require a different object from the beauties of nature'. To *melt into tears* has passed into prosaic diction. But surely no prose could venture upon so bold a metaphor as 'My lonely anguish melts my heart'.

And in my breast th' imperfect joys expire.

This is a very poetical and metaphorical periphrasis for saying that the joys of spring are imperfect to the writer, because they are confined to his own breast, and not partaken by his departed friend. No prose letter, except such an one as should be modelled upon Dr Johnson's Essay on Letter-writing in the Rambler,[168] instead of this, could say; 'My imperfect joys expire in my own breast'. That, even without the inversion of the words, is not only the thought, but the language, of poetry; or poetic diction. If Mr Gray had written it in a letter, he would have added, as he humorously did on one occasion: 'This sentence is so fine, I am quite ashamed; but no matter; you must translate it into prose'.

The last two lines only are a just illustration of Mr Wordsworth's theory, and show that very strong passion in verse can afford to use the language of prose; but lighter emotions and fanciful descriptions had better not despise the accomplishment of poetic diction. [Mr Gifford in his Quarterly Review of this Preface (vol. xiv p. 906) made some sensible remarks on this Critique of Gray's Sonnet, and on poetic diction in general. 'The sun ⟨he says⟩ is the *golden fire of reddening Phoebus* ... it is doing Mr Wordsworth himself nothing more than justice to say, that, in his happier hours of inspiration, when his theories and eccentricities happen to be laid aside, no writer of the day seems to understand better the exact key, in which the language of this last kind of poetry should be pitched'.]

Let not verbal criticism too much divert us from the argument of this sonnet, the moral of which is very unsatisfactory; and therefore is the poem faulty in a higher sense. Some brighter hope should surely have been held out, at the close of it, than this heathen paradox; for it

[168] *Rambler* No. 152, *Works*, Yale edn, Vol. V, pp. 42-7.

was first said by Solon, on the death of his son. But with all his taste and feeling, Gray had little imagination. Let us hear how Mr Wordsworth moralizes upon a similar subject:

> Thus might he paint our lot of mortal days,
> Who wants the glorious faculty, assign'd
> To elevate the more than reasoning mind,
> And colour life's dark cloud with orient rays.
> Imagination is that sacred power,
> Imagination lofty and refin'd:
> 'Tis hers to pluck the amaranthine flower
> Of Faith, and round the sufferer's temples bind
> Wreaths that endure Affliction's heaviest shower,
> And do not shrink from Sorrow's keenest wind.

[*Misc. Sonnets*, I, xxxv, ll. 5-14, III, 20]

And how different from Gray, is the conclusion of Milton's monody on the death of *his* friend! . . .[169] [Dr Beattie originally published his 'Hermit', ending with the following lines—

> But when shall Spring visit the mouldering urn?
> Oh, when shall it dawn on the night of thy grave?

But he afterwards added the two Stanzas, which now so happily conclude the poem.[170]] If Mr Gray considered a future state of existence too sacred a subject to be introduced into so short a poem, there were other poetical consolations, as in the following still shorter dirge by Collins, in which I shall take the liberty of transposing the fourth couplet to the second place, not only because that is the more natural order of the sense; but also because such an arrangement avoids the clash between '*their* knell, *their* dirge', and 'there Honour'. . . . How simple! how exquisite! how profound! And this is the poetry, which, according to Dr Johnson, 'may extort praise, when it gives little pleasure'.[171]

CHAPTER IX   To proceed with Mr Wordsworth's theory,—The great mass of his poetry is as much enchased with poetic diction, in the best sense of the word, as that even of Pope or Gray. The language of his later poems is, in my opinion, almost too exquisite, and proves the

[169] Field here quotes *Lycidas*, ll. 165-81.
[170] *Poetical Works*, ed. Alexander Dyce, London 1866, pp. 95-6, ll. 31-2, 33-48.
[171] 'Ode, Written in the Beginning of the Year 1746', *Poetical Works of Gray and Collins*, p. 258; Johnson, *Lives*, Vol. III, p. 341.

truth of his friend Mr Coleridge's observation, that 'impassioned, lofty and sustained diction is the characteristic of his genius'.[172] I cannot resist the pleasure of giving an example of this, in the last two stanzas of a very favorite poem of mine—The Brownie's Cell—. It seems to me that nothing can be more select and Shaksperian than the diction as well as the thought (the romantic illustrated by the classical) of these consummate verses: [ll. 81-100, III, 97] . . . What a richness of impasto! How the rhyme fetches out the flavour of the fruit, like sugar! These verses are quite equal to Milton's L'Allegro and Il Penseroso. I prefer Mr Wordsworth's Odes (as I will call them) to his Sonnets, certainly to his minor blank-verse effusions, except perhaps the Lines on a Portrait ['Lines Suggested by a Portrait from the Pencil of F. Stone', IV, 120-4]. In blank verse, all poets are too apt to take up with the first word the mind suggests, which, though it is said to be the right one in prose, is certainly not in poetry. In the sonnets the rhymes are rung upon too common words. Difficult rhymes make the poet cast about for another word or idea; and second thoughts, which are best, generally reward him with a more picturesque turn or word, yet, if victorious, equally easy and simple in appearance.

But what the Preface to the Lyrical Ballads means, and what was then so necessary to be taught, is, that it is the poetry that must make the diction, and not only not the diction the poetry, but that true poetry is quite independant of any traditional or conventional diction. The poet's pen gives to airy nothing a local habitation; but it must not be in the cuckoo-nest of another's architecture, but spun, as it were, out of its own bowels,

> Like that fine worm that doth inter
> Herself in the silken sepulchre.[173]

I have always thought that it was one of the boasts of the English language over the French, that it had a poetic diction, which the French language has not. This diction does not consist in well-precedented epithet or in hereditary circumlocution—in calling the sea the *liquid road* or the *briny wave*, or the nightingale the *Attic warbler* or *Philomel*, which are what Mr Wordsworth is so justly disgusted with in Pope's Homer and Gray's Odes, but still in metaphorical language, and not in that of colloquial prose. A *selection* of the language usually spoken by men, Mr Wordsworth allows; and that selection is to pick out all the most figurative and picturesque phrases of our rich

---

[172] *Biog. Lit.*, Vol. II, p. 6.
[173] Herrick, 'Upon a Flie', ll. 13-14, *Poetical Works*, ed. L. C. Martin, Oxford 1956, p. 185.

language; and these constitute what, in a good sense, is called poetic diction. The best explanation of the phrase, that I know of, occurs in the following passage from Johnson's Life of Dryden, however incorrect the fact may be, as applied to that poet:—

'There was, before the time of Dryden, no poetical diction, no system of words, at once refined from the grossness of domestic use, and free from the harshness of terms appropriated to particular arts. . . . We had few elegancies or flowers of speech; the roses had not yet been plucked from the brambles; or different colours had not been joined to enliven one another.'[174]

For myself (and, thanks to the gradual influence of the Lyrical Ballads, the public taste has long been slowly but surely coming round to my opinion), so far from objecting to the homeliness of Mr Wordsworth's diction upon homely subjects, I like the earlier editions of his poems better than the later ones, in which I am sorry to say that our preface-writer has not kept faith with his old disciples, but has paid a deference to Mr Jeffrey's Edinburgh Review, which it ill deserved. In the Preface from which I have hitherto quoted so largely, is the following passage:

'I am sensible that my associations must have sometimes been particular, instead of general . . . But it is dangerous to make these alterations on the single authority of a few individuals . . . since they are so much less interested in the subject, they may decide lightly and carelessly.' [II, 402]

There is a great deal of truth in this; but hear the other side: 'It is a question variously disputed ⟨says Dryden⟩ whether an author may be allowed as a competent judge of his own works . . . fancy, if I may so speak, judging of itself, can be no more certain or demonstrative of its own effects, than two crooked lines can be the adequate measure of each other'.

'What is good only because it pleases ⟨adds Dr Johnson⟩ cannot be pronounced good till it has been found to please'.[175]

The appeal, after all, is to Time, who is a better judge than even the poet, the critic being the worst of all . . .[176]

Of the poem, entitled 'The Beggars', Mr Jeffrey was pleased to say that there was something about it, that convinced him that it was a

---

[174] *Lives*, Vol. I, p. 420.
[175] Preface to *Secret Love, Works of John Dryden*, ed. H. T. Swedenborg *et al.*, California 1966, Vol. IX, p. 115; *Lives*, Vol. I, p. 340 (a comment on this Preface).
[176] Field here quotes Dryden's comments on hasty and judicious critics in the Dedication to *Aureng-Zebe, Dramatic Works*, ed. Montague Summers, 6 vols, London 1931-2, Vol. IV, p. 85.

favorite of the author's, though to him it appeared to be a very paragon of silliness and affectation. In a subsequent edition of his poem Mr Wordsworth altered the diction of this piece, in my opinion, unnecessarily; and I am glad to see that in the latest edition, the poet has restored some of its simplicity. It will afford an useful lesson to the poetical student, to compare the three editions of this poem; and such comparison will at least prove the author's want of tenacity, and that 'The Beggars' was not such a favorite as Mr Jeffrey charges, but that its parent could bear to correct it; but correction does not always improve the offspring. *Manum de tabula* is sometimes the better precept; *Poliat lima non exterat* . . .[177]

Of the true story of the 'Blind Highland Boy', launching himself on an arm of the sea, in a washing-tub, Mr Jeffrey said that 'the introduction of this *household tub* was carrying the matter as far as it would well go, and that there was nothing, down to the wiping of shoes, or the evisceration of chickens, which might not be introduced into poetry if this was tolerated'.[178] There is nothing, however homely, that may not be introduced into poetry, if the mind be properly prepared for it, and the result be pleasurable. Poetry is like the sun, 'a god, kissing carrion',[179] as Shakspeare calls him. It is customary to take a distinction between weeds and flowers; but even weeds bear flowers. [The only question is whether the word be necessary to the argument, and whether the argument be worthy of poetry. On neither of these points can there be any doubt in the case of the Blind Highland Boy. It is a tale most pregnant with poetry, and the tub was essential to it.] . . .[180]

---

[177] Field here sets out in parallel the 1807 (which he calls the 1815), 1827 and 1837 texts of the poem (see II, 222-4). He notes that 'a weed of glorious feature', l. 18, is from Spenser (*Muiopotmos*, l. 213—de Selincourt).

[178] Edinburgh Review, vol. XI, p. 225. In the debate on the copyright act of the year 1842 a second Jeffrey arose in the person of Mr Wakley who read for scorn aloud in the House several of Mr Wordsworth's ballad-poems, contending that such things were unworthy of legal protection; but he was more than 30 years too late. Even in the uncongenial atmosphere of the House of Commons, the poems were listened to, and the scorn and laughter were long afterwards retorted upon Mr Wakley himself, through both the periodical and the permanent press [BF]. Comment on 1842 debate added later.

[179] *Hamlet*, II. ii. 182, 'If the sun breed maggots in a dead dog, being a good [? god] kissing carrion'.

[180] At this point Field embarks on a rambling justification of his thesis with various illustrations, several added later. Although some interesting points are made these pages stray too far to be worth giving in full. The discussion takes in the notion of a 'Flemish school of poetry' which includes Chaucer, Crabbe and Burns; brief reference to Theocritus and Virgil; mention of W. L. Bowles's *Two Letters to Lord Byron* . . . [*on*] *Pope*, London 1821; defences of ll. 116-7 of Gray's *Progress of Poesy*, *Poems*, p. 16, and of a passage from Dyer's *The Fleece*, Book I, ll. 210-13, *Poems*, p. 53 ('That is poetry, though Dr

In the poem of the Blind Highland Boy, in the same manner as with Lady Macbeth's *knife*, the passion elevates the accidents. 'In all that truly merits the name of poetry, in its most comprehensive sense ⟨says Mr Coleridge⟩, there is a necessary predominance of the ideas, that is, of that which originates in the artist himself, and a comparative indifference of the materials'.[181] The poet is the maker. It is the poet that makes the poetical; and not the poetical the poet. Let Mr Jeffrey look at Wilkie's picture of the Princess Doria, washing the feet of the pilgrims. He will there see a common household tub introduced; yet nobody but what Addison calls 'your little buffoon reader' would think this ridiculous. The action is elevated by the Christian charity of the subject. *Et vos debetis alter alterius lavare pedes.*

[Verbis ea vincere magnum
Quam sit, et angustis hunc addire rebus honorem.
—Virgilius.]

Sir David Wilkie might have substituted for this tub the silver basin and ewer, which the Princess has near her; but he felt that such a *turtle-shell* would have been out of keeping with the poor pilgrim and would have deducted from the sincere humiliation of the action. For, I am sorry to say, that, instead of practising his precept, which I have before quoted, Mr Wordsworth in a subsequent edition of his Poems, 'in deference to the opinion of a friend [Coleridge] substituted a turtle-shell for the less elegant vessel, in which his blind voyager did actually

---

Johnson could see nothing in The Fleece'); praise of Warton as 'the father of modern poetical criticism' and of his comments on Pope's 'Man of Ross' passage; mention of Currie's notes on Burns's correspondence, in the second volume of his edition of the *Works*, 3 vols, Liverpool 1800; allusion to Voltaire's 'verbal commentaries' on Corneille; and, probably most importantly, fairly closely argued objections to Johnson's well-known comments on *Macbeth*, I, v, 48-52 in *Rambler* No. 168, *Works*, Vol. V, p. 128. Horace, Spenser, Milton, Boileau, Fielding, Pope, Thomson, Shenstone, Collins, Campbell, Jeffrey, Lamb, Coleridge and of course Wordsworth are all also mentioned or quoted briefly. On Johnson and *Macbeth* Field has no difficulty in finding examples in major poets of 'dun' and 'knife', and he suggests the '"blanket of the dark", associated as it is here, with murdering a man in his bed, is little different from the curtain of the dark'. Overall, 'I can only say that I firmly believe nobody ever felt any other emotion, than that of awe at this passage. ... I cannot call this an instance of poetry, debased by mean expressions; and see nothing in the whole speech but the language of Nature.'

[181] I cannot find an exact source for this characteristically Coleridgean remark; Field could have heard it in conversation or at a lecture, or it may be his imperfect recollection of a sentence in *Biog. Lit.*

entrust himself to the dangerous current of Loch Levin'.[182] By this means, to be sure, he gained the following beautiful stanza in describing the boat-party, which went in pursuit of the poor blind tub-sailor: [ll. 191-5, III, 94.] . . . But still I (for one) preferred the old homely fact; and wish the 'household tub' had been restored, as well as the Beggars 'telling a lie' [l. 44, II, 224; see 1836-40 reading].

These temporary clamours should never be yielded to, by a man of genius. So the outcry of *pedlar* was raised against the fine poem of the Excursion, because the author took for the principal interlocutor in that philosophical dialogue (not unworthy of Plato) an old man who had once followed that calling in the north country. Even Mr Hazlitt, an admirer of the poem, says that 'he takes leave of the poet, when he makes pedlars and ploughmen his heroes, and the interpreters of his sentiments. It is ⟨he thinks⟩ getting into low company, and company, besides, that he does not like. He is satisfied with the friendship that subsisted between Parson Adams and Joseph Andrews'.[183] I do not know which of the persons in the Excursion Mr Hazlitt calls a plough-man. The other two are or have been clergymen. But I know that Burns was a ploughman. Was he low company? Mr Hazlitt was a man to have left princes and dukes, to have supped with him. He admits that Joseph Andrews was not a vulgar person, although Fielding intended him as a burlesque upon Pamela. Mr Wordsworth's hero is a higher man than Pamela Andrews' father. Time has consecrated Joseph Andrews, and Goodman Andrews, and Mrs Andrews; and Time will equally ennoble Mr Wordsworth's retired pedlar, 'that old man eloquent'.[184] Mr Lamb, in his critique of the Excursion, in the Quarterly Review, justly says that 'the poet's plan required a character in humble life to be the organ of his philosophy. It was in harmony with the system and scenery of his poem.'[185] It may be added that the plan also required a hero, who should not only have been the confidant of every cottager's family, but who should also have extended his visits over a wide circle of country: the circuit of a village medical practitioner would not have been large enough, and his rank would have been too high. Nobody but a pedlar would have suited the poet's purpose; and may this fine old reality never be changed into the finical abstraction of a *palmer* or *pilgrim*, as Mr Lamb recommends to those who feel scandalized at a name. But, as the poet says of another hero,

[182] Wordsworth's note, III, 96. See also Wordsworth's comment in letter of 24 April 1828. *Letters, Later Years*, I, 307-13, and above, Ch. III.
[183] 'On Mr Wordsworth's Excursion', *Complete Works*, Vol. IV, p. 120.
[184] Milton [BF]. Sonnet X, l. 8.
[185] *Works*, Vol. I, p. 199.

'Twas not for the unfeeling, the falsely refin'd,
The squeamish in taste and the narrow of mind,
And the small critic, wielding his delicate pen,
That he sang of the Pedlar, the pride of old men.

['The Farmer of Tilsbury Vale', ll. 1-4, IV, 240]

[Mr Hartley Coleridge who inherits much of the genius of his father once observed to me that he thought the hero of the Excursion should not have been a pedlar, unless it had been the poet's plan to show the prosperity of natural wisdom or self-education in humble life. But, he said, many of the Pedlar's observations are far too refined for even such a character. How is it possible to predicate this, when we so often see genius and philosophy spring out of the ground (as it were)? It *was* a part of the poet's plan to show that 'with the lowly is wisdom';[186] and this is the main ingredient in the character of the whole of Wordsworth's poetry. The hero of the Excursion, like Burns, was not an uneducated person. He was not such a scholar as his fore-runner Mr John Brown.[187] That learned divine had a natural turn for languages: the bent of the Pedlar of the poem was towards reflexion—to imagination—to human wisdom—to philosophy. He needed not to go to schools or colleges for this, like Mr Brown. The world was his congenial university—Man and Nature were his proper studies.]

'The genius of Mr Wordsworth ⟨Mr Hazlitt beautifully says⟩ was not a spirit that descended to him through the air: it sprang out of the ground like a flower.'[188] How ⟨asked Ulysses, addressing his guardian goddess⟩ shall I be able to recognize Proteus in the swallow that skims round our houses, when I have been accustomed to behold him as a swan of Phoebus, measuring his movements to a celestial music? In both alike ⟨she replied⟩ thou can'st recognize the god.

---

[186] Proverbs, xi. 2 [BF].

[187] 'Soon after he abandoned the occupation of a shepherd, and undertook that of pedlar or travelling merchant. This mode of life was once of much greater importance and higher estimation in Scotland, than at present, when the facilities of communication between all parts of the country and the greater seats of commerce have been so immensely multiplied, and was often pursued by persons of great intelligence and respectability.' *Memoir of the Rev. John Brown, Author of the Self-interpreting Bible*. [BF]. I have not seen this model for the Pedlar suggested elsewhere. Wordsworth himself mentioned James Patrick of Kendal, 'the intellectual Pedlar' (I.F. note, V, 373-4).

[188] *Complete Works*, Vol. XVII, p. 117.

CHAPTER X   It is not my intention, as Dr Warton has done towards
Pope, to examine every one of Mr Wordsworth's poems [or rather,
since the Doctor has criticised Pope in a severe spirit, to become my
Poet's Owen Ruffhead, that heavy lawyer who defended each poem
of Pope from Warton's criticisms[189]]. The dates of Mr Wordsworth's
compositions will be found affixed to nearly the whole of them, from
which it will be seen which were the Lyrical Ballads, and which were
subsequent works. In the edition of 1815, the poet for the first time
classed them all under the[se] heads . . . Such of the above heads as are
subjective afford a useful classification; but such as are objective
cannot so well be confined to the respective boundaries of the affections,
the fancy, the imagination, the reflection. Mr Wordsworth was aware
of this, and tells us that these objective poems 'are placed according to
the powers of the mind, in the author's conception, predominant in
the production. . . . The most striking productions of each piece,
mutual illustration, variety and proportion, have governed me through-
out' [1815 Preface, II, 434] . . .[190] This preface, however, contains a
lecture on poetry, quite as philosophical and beautiful, as that to the
Lyrical Ballads, and the discrimination therein contained, between
fancy and imagination, is very admirable, although the illustration
from Shakspeare's

> half way down
> *Hangs* one who gathers samphire,

may be called unfortunate, since the samphire-gatherer does not
metaphorically but literally hang. 'It is terrible ⟨says Smith, in his
History of Waterford, 1774⟩ to see how people gather it, hanging by
a rope several fathoms from the top of the impending rocks, as it were
in the air'. *As it were, in the air*: that is the poet's point—that his
imagination seizes; but Shakspeare appears likewise to have known

[189] And yet I cannot help, lawyer-like, saying a word on behalf of Ruffhead's
Life of Pope. It is, after all, the great fountain of the poet's biography; it is the
Life that Warburton, the poet's literary executor, promised in his edition of
Pope's works; and a very great part of it is evidently written by the Bishop,
though he was then too proud a prelate and preferred to employ another hand
which could eulogize him as well as Pope. Many of Mr Ruffhead's reclamations
from J. Warton are very just: Warburton would not have intrusted 'the
original manuscripts from which the work was compiled' to a fool: and I
should like to know how many other editors of the Statutes at Large could
write such a book, one 'leisure vacation' [BF].
[190] After listing the 'heads' and quoting the 1815 Preface, Field briefly suggests
that in later editions many poems were 'more satisfactorily removed to other
heads', although there remained 'several poems *incertae sedis*, as there always
must be in every classification, however scientific and however minute'.

that the samphire-gatherer does literally hang; for he adds—'dreadful trade!'.

Mr Wordsworth's six volumes [1836-7] open with the well-known nine lines

My heart leaps up, when I behold . . . [I, 226]

of which Mr Jeffrey says, 'This is the whole'. I answer, And what a whole! *Quam multa, quam paucis*! What a summary of all the poetry of life, and how simply, and yet exquisitely expressed! It is well placed, as the motto and scope, 'the be-all and end-all' of the six volumes.

The seventh poem is 'Alice Fell' [I, 232], of which I agree with Mr Coleridge, that there is no sufficient cause for its being recorded in metre,[191] and whenever I used to lend my volume, I pasted it down, a very simple way of disposing of what one does not like, and a practice which does oneself and others much more good than scorn and mockery.

The tenth is the beautiful 'Anecdote for Fathers' [I, 241], illustrating the proverb of 'Ask me no questions, and I'll tell you no lies'. 'That authority ⟨says Mrs Barbauld, who knew the hearts of children as well as anybody, though perhaps her little books minister too little to their imagination⟩ which extends its claims over every action and over every thought, which insists upon an answer to every interrogatory, however indiscreet or oppressive to the feelings, will, in young or old, produce falsehood.'[192] Retine vim istam; falsa enim dicam si coges.[193]

In the last of the 'Poems, referring to the period of Childhood', which is the sublimest lyric of the whole, there is only one inversion of language,

While thy brow youth's roses crown.

['The Longest Day', l. 68 (1836-7, cf. 1845), I, 249]

I think this kind of mortuary poetry scarcely admits of inversions; and I cannot help wishing this only one were altered. There is also a slight clash between *brow* and *crown*. [In the poem entitled 'Descriptive Sketches' is the following line.

There an old man an *olden* measure scann'd.

[l. 147, I, 53]

Old and *olden* are the singular and plural of the same word. It sounds too much like old and older. Perhaps that would be better.]

---

[191] *Biog. Lit.*, Vol. II, p. 53.

[192] 'On Education', *The Works of Mrs. Barbauld*, 2 vols, London 1825, Vol. II, pp. 311-12.

[193] Iusebius, lib. VI, Praepar. Evang. c. 1 [BF].

The cast of the twelfth poem of the Affections [II, 31, 'Look at the fate . . .'] reminds me of my old favorite, Herrick: it is equally sweet in sentiment with his best poems, and far deeper in thought. Clergyman as Herrick was, there is no more moral in his lyrics than Anacreon or Horace had taught him. None but religious poetry can be immortal[194] —according to the measure of the light vouchsafed, Heathen or Christian. [How much grander would have been Pope's Essay on Man, had he taken Dr Young's advice!

> O! had he press'd his theme, pursued the track
> Which opens out of darkness into day!
> O! had he mounted on his wing of fire,
> Soar'd when I sink, and sung immortal man![195]

On account of this defect, even Dryden's *Religio Laici* with all its poetical inferiority, is more satisfactory reading than the Essay on Man. The fact is, Pope, like every other poet knew where his strength lay, and that he could soar no higher. Dr Young's praise is very creditable to his modesty; for, with all his paradox and sophistry, the Night Thoughts do not sink, but grandly sing immortal man; and the same writer's satires are nearly equal to Pope's.]

Parallel with the third stanza of the next poem:

> O! what a weight is in these shades! Ye leaves . . .

> ['Tis said, that some have died for love', ll. 21-8, II, 33]

I would quote, in illustration of the truth of this sentiment, the follow-ing exquisite passage from Burns:—

> Ye banks and braes o' bonnie Doon . . .[196]

[Poetry cannot go beyond this; but while yet in early England she sung, Shakspeare, when young, had the same idea:—

> The little birds that tune their morning's joy . . .[197]]

It is said of Michael, in the poem of that name [II, 80] that he left the sheep-fold unfinished when he died. Am I right in conjecturing, that the poet meant this, in order that the son might not be said to have broken the covenant with his father to lead a virtuous life?

---

[194] See Remains of Alexander Knox Esq. Vol. III, p. 354 [BF].
[195] *Night Thoughts*, Night I, ll. 456-9, *Young's Complete Works*, ed. James Nichols, 2 vols, London 1854, Vol. I, p. 13.
[196] 'The Banks o' Doon' (B), ll. 1-18, *Poems and Songs*, ed. James Kinsley, 3 vols, Oxford 1968, Vol. III, p. 575.
[197] *The Rape of Lucrece*, ll. 1107-15, 1121-7.

The 'Waggoner' [II, 176] is a very natural, pleasing poem, in the style of Gainsborough or Morland, such as will always find admirers. Thomson coloured more gorgeously; but the following passage from the Seasons would furnish a very dignified motto for the English story:—

> Beneath descending hills, the caravan
> Is buried deep. In Cairo's crowded streets
> The impatient merchant, wond'ring, waits in vain,
> And Mecca saddens at the long delay.[198]

Twelfth poem of the Fancy:

> Thou must needs, I think, have had
> Celandine! and long ago
> Praise of which I nothing know.
>
> ['To the Same Flower', ll. 6-8, II, 144]

I can find none but in Cowley's 'Plants', in which there are two poems on the Celandine—on its medical virtues alone. The following line affords the only coincidence with Mr Wordsworth:

> The gaudy Spring by thy approach is known.[199]

The twenty-fourth poem of the Fancy ['The Poet and the Caged Turtledove', II, 163] is an exquisite gem, which I would venture to set in the following motto:—

> Whether the Muse or Love call thee his mate,
> Both them I serve, and of their train am I.[200]

May I be permitted to remove a little flaw in the cutting of this jewel? ... [ll. 9-12] 'I rather think' is too colloquial for so elegant a stanza: Read—

> I rather deem the gentle Dove,   &c.   &c.   &c.[201]

[This poem always reminds me of Cowper's happy stanzas 'To the Nightingale which the author heard sing on New Year's Day'.[202] To

---

[198] The poet told me he would adopt this [BF]. Written in later, apparently hastily. *The Seasons*, 'Summer', ll. 976-9, *Poetical Works*, ed. J. L. Robertson, Oxford 1908, p. 88.

[199] *Works*, 3 vols, London 1721, Vol. III, p. 282 (tr. of *Plantarum*, 1662). The 'coincidence' is not very close.

[200] Milton, 'O Nightingale!', ll. 13-14.

[201] Mr Wordsworth did not agree with me here [BF]. Written in later, apparently hastily.

[202] *Poetical Works*, p. 414.

dispose of all my verbal criticisms at once, let me collect the rest of the lines, which I consider as too prosaic or colloquial. 'What wonder if a poet *now and then*.' 'One of the Norton tenantry.' 'With proof before her that on public ends Domestic virtue vitally depends.' 'And the broad gulphs, I travers'd oft and oft.' ['When I have borne in memory ...', l. 12, III, 118; *The White Doe of Rylstone*, l. 1506, III, 329; 'The Warning', ll. 74-5, IV, 110;[203] 'Epitaphs translated from Chiabrera', IV, l. 17, IV, 250.]]

Second poem of the Imagination:

> O Cuckoo! shall I call thee Bird,
> Or but a wandering Voice?
>
> ['To the Cuckoo', ll. 3-4, II, 207]

This was said by Lipsius of the Nightingale: *Vox est—præterea nihil*; and I don't think the quotation, which is in everybody's mouth, can be attributed higher.

Seventh poem of the Imagination ['O Nightingale', II, 214]. Pliny says of the nightingale: *Tanta vox tam parvo in corpusculo! tam pertinax spiritus.*

In the ninth, there is a parallel idea in Suckling's poems ['A slumber did my spirit seal ...', II, 216] ...

> Heaven! shall this fresh ornament of the world,
> These precious love-lines, pass with common things,
> Among the wastes of time? What pity 'twere.[204]

The next poem has been imitated by Mr Montgomery in his 'Little Cloud':

> ['I wandered lonely as a cloud', II, 216, ll. 17-24] ...
> Amidst the cares, the toils, the strife,
> The weariness and waste of life,
> That day shall memory oft restore,
> And in a moment live it o'er,
> When with a lightening flash of thought,
> Morn, noon and we at once are brought
> (As thro' the vision of a trance)
> All in the compass of a glance.[205]

[203] Wordsworth altered l. 74 for 1840 edn.
[204] From the play *Brennoralt*, III. iv. 25-8, *Works of Suckling; Plays*, ed. L. A. Beaurline, Oxford 1971, p. 216.
[205] *Poetical Works*, Vol. III, p. 161.

The nineteenth poem, 'The Thorn' [II, 240-8], seems to be founded on Bürger's ballad of The Parson's Daughter with these differences, that the parson's daughter certainly murders her natural child; but it is *her* ghost, and not the baby's, that haunts its grave, which she had torn, according to Mr William Taylor's translation,

> With bleeding nails, beside the pond,
> And nightly pines the pool beside.[206]

The true story of 'Goody Blake and Harry Gill' [IV, 173] is related in Darwin's Zoonomia, as follows . . .[207]

[Mr Coleridge, at a subsequent period, wrote a still more unpleasant ballad upon a similar subject, entitled 'The Three Graves'. My friend Richard Cargill, himself a West Indian, afterwards published a 'Poem on the Superstition of Obeah', in which the curse of the wicked found a more probable scene for its poetical material than a Christian country.[208] I cannot call to mind without delight the days, when this (now deceased) gentleman, Mr Serjeant Talfourd and I were fellow-pupils in a special pleader's office, in which, though law was the idol, literature was respected, and poetry unridiculed.

Mr Wordsworth one day said to me:— 'It is not enough for a poet to possess the power of mind; he must also have knowledge of the heart, and this can only be acquired by time and tranquil leisure. No great poem has been written by a young man or by an unhappy one. It was poor dear Coleridge's constant infelicity that prevented him from being the poet that Nature had given him the power to be. He had always too much personal and domestic discontent to paint the sorrows of mankind. He could not

> afford to suffer
> With those whom he saw suffer.

> [*The Excursion*, Bk I, ll. 370-1, V, 20]

I gave him the subject of his Three Graves; but he made it too shocking and painful, and not sufficiently sweetened by any healing views. Not being able to dwell on or sanctify natural woes, he took to the super-natural, and hence his Antient Mariner and Christabel, in which he

---

[206] de Selincourt notes that Taylor's translation was published in the *Monthly Magazine* in 1796. He suggests that a Scots ballad is a more likely source (II, 513-14).

[207] Field here quotes from *Zoonomia, or the Laws of Organic Life*, 2 vols, London 1794-6; the passage is given by de Selincourt, IV, 439-40.

[208] Cargill was a Jamaican who studied under Rough and also Thelwall. He afterwards became a clergyman. *Corr. HCR*, Vol. I, p. 85 n. 2. I cannot trace the poem.

shows great poetical power; but these things have not the hold on the heart which Nature gives, and will never be popular, like Goldsmith's or Burns's'.[209]]

Mr Wordsworth, like Shakspeare, is equally excellent in the classical, as the romantic. I cannot pass the poem of 'Laodamia', [II, 267], without acknowledging the improvement it has received, in consequence of the criticisms of Mr Landor, in his 'Imaginary Conversation' between Southey and Porson, to which I would refer the reader, as to a noble testimonial to the genius of Wordsworth. A writer in the Quarterly Review for April, 1837 (perhaps Mr Southey) says that 'Mr Wordsworth, in his late castigated edition of his poetry, has divested several of the finest pieces in the collection (the peerless Laodamia, for example) of some of their charms'. Now, with the exception of a correction of the facts of the story, the only alterations the poet made in Laodamia are those required by Mr Landor . . .[210]

[There is no doubt that the religion of Jesus Christ ought not to be mixed up with the heathen mythology. It is like the Emperor Constantine's crowning the Statue of Apollo with the supposed nails of the Cross, instead of rays. But] the language in question [ll. 101-2] (it may be observed) is equally that of the church and the conventicle: it is the language of scripture. [Nevertheless it is justly remarked by Mr Foster, in his Essay on the Aversion of Men of Taste to Evangelical Religion,[211] the Christian writer or speaker ought, instead of always using the technical term, occasionally to express at length, in other words, even at the expense of much circumlocution, the idea which he would have wished to convey had he used the peculiar term.] The Quarterly Review (for February, 1837) admits that the expression *second birth*, being appropriated to the exposition of a Christian doctrine, was not fortunately chosen, but sees no objection to the word *witness*. It would not have been objectionable but for its society, which (say not, contaminates it, Mr Landor, but) communicates to it the odour of sanctity. Mr Wordsworth was accordingly wise enough to alter the concluding couplet [of the stanza] thus [ll. 101-2; cf. 1815-20 text] . . . This is a golden couplet indeed; and one for the opportunity of disclosing which, the author ought for ever to be obliged to his really poetic critic. Now the religion both seems and is all of a piece;

[209] For Wordsworth's and Coleridge's parts in *The Three Graves*, see I, 374, and Moorman, *The Early Years*, pp. 388-9.

[210] See Appendix No. III [BF]. de Selincourt, II, 519, nn. to ll. 1-6 and 101-2, also gives Landor's criticisms of the early readings, i.e. of similar line endings and of words inappropriately 'stinking and reeking from the conventicle'.

[211] John Foster, in *Essays in a Series of Letters . . .*, 2 vols, London 1805, Vol. II, pp. 98-297.

and the employment of the Hero in the Shades is derived from the same exquisite book of Virgil, in which we read of Laodamia herself:

> Quæ gratia currum
> Armorumque fuit vivis, quæ cura nitentis
> Pascere equos, eadem sequitur tellure repostos.

In like manner, it may be remarked that the word *rites* in the following Sonnet XXIII of the River Duddon, connected with *laving*, suggests a Christian sacrament, which is only profaned by any allusion to it here:

> the fervour of the year
> Pour'd on the fleece-encumber'd flock, invites
> To laving currents for prelusive rites
> Duly perform'd, before the Dalesmen shear
> Their panting charge.

> > [ll. 1-5 (1820-43), III, 255]

The whole diction here is too graced for the occasion: the third line is in Latin.[212]

I would presume to suggest one more polish of the poem of Laodamia:

> That thou should'st cheat the malice of the grave

'Should'st *cheat*' is hardly utterable. Say

> Thou should'st elude the malice of the grave.[213]

> > [l. 58 (1815-36 reading above)]

'Laodamia' had previously formed the subject of an elegy by Mrs West,[214] one of the poetesses of the dark age of Mr Hayley, Miss Seward, Mr Jermingham, Miss More, Mrs Carter, Mr Merry, &c. &c. &c. upon which the stars of Cowper, Burns, Southey, Wordsworth and Coleridge rose but the lady's verse only knows that the ghost of Protesilaus appeared to his wife the night after his death and that she died to join him, and even the Elegy omits the point that

> the Delphic oracle foretold
> That the first Greek who touch'd the Trojan strand
> Should die.

> > [ll. 43-5, II, 268]

---

[212] In consequence of these objections the Poet altered the passage as follows: ...[1845 text] [BF].

[213] de Selincourt (II, 519) notes a letter from Field in November 1839 making this point.

[214] 'Elegy I', *Poems*, York 1791, pp. 34-41.

In the poem of 'Peter Bell', in the space between the description of the hero and the commencement of the tale, I have, in my copy, transcribed the following stanza from Gray's Long Story, the style of which, in narration, Mr Wordsworth has here happily imitated; but his poem goes far deeper into the human heart, than any poem of Gray's:

> What in the very first beginning?
> Shame of the versifying tribe!
> Your history whither are you spinning?
> Can you do nothing but describe?[215]

That fits it well.

In the first part of the Miscellaneous Sonnets, XII, is the following striking coincidence:

> I have no pain that calls for patience, no;
> Hence am I cross and peevish as a child.

[ll. 9-10, III, 8]

'Et c'est encore ce que me fache, de n'être pas même en droit de me facher.' Nouvelle Heloise, p. 6.

[For the XXXIIId of these Sonnets [III, 18] I would suggest the following motto:— 'I had rather believe all the fables in the Legend and the Talmud and the Koran than that this universal frame is without a mind'.—Bacon.[216]]

Among the Memorials of a Tour in Scotland in 1803, is a poem to a Highland Girl, the conclusion of which [ll. 72-8, III, 75] is imitated by the last lines of Mr Rogers's 'Loch Long' . . .[217] So does the opening of Mr Rogers's 'Boy of Egremond' echo that of Mr Wordsworth's 'Force of Prayer' [IV, 88]—the story being the same . . .[218]

Yarrow Visited, 1st edition [1815]

> Yon cottage seems a bower of bliss;
> It promises protection
> To studious ease, and generous cares
> And every chaste affection.

---

[215] 'A Long Story', ll. 17-20, *Poems*, p. 44. Field probably means between the Prologue and Part First, II, 388-9. I do not recall seeing this comparison made elsewhere.

[216] de Selincourt (III, 424) notes a letter from Field of 17 December 1836 suggesting this motto.

[217] 'Written in the Highlands of Scotland, September 2, 1812' ('Loch Long'), last six lines, *Poetical Works*, London 1875, p. 174.

[218] *Poetical Works*, p. 171. Field also notices Wordsworth's use here of Logan's 'Braes of Yarrow', quoting the relevant lines; see de Selincourt's n. to ll. 39-40, *app. crit.*, IV, 421.

Charles Lamb objected that this literary resident was out of keeping, like a painter intruding himself, sitting on a camp stool with his portfolio, into a romantic landskip. The poet accordingly altered the stanza thus: [ll. 62-4, III, 107] . . .[219]

The idea of the first Sonnet of the Memorials of a Tour on the Continent is evidently taken from Hogarth's Gates of Calais, where the fish called *maids* are made to resemble the fish-women:— [III, 164, ll. 1-9] . . . [220]

For the Elegiac Stanzas, on the death of Frederick William Goddard [III, 193], I beg to offer the following motto from Cowley:—

> Whether some brave young man's untimely fate,
> In *words worth dying for*, he celebrate,
> Such mournful and such flowing words,
> As joy to his mother's grief affords; —
> The grave can but the dross of him devour;
> So small is Death's, so great the Poet's power.[221]

Among the Poems of Sentiment and Reflection, is one entitled 'Fidelity' [IV, 80-3], founded, like Sir Walter Scott's 'Helvellyn', upon the following incident, as related by Bishop Watson, in a letter to Mr Hayley: 'On one of our highest mountains (Helvellyn) a man was lost last year ⟨1804⟩. Two months after his disappearance ⟨the poet says three, Mr de Quincey five or six⟩ his body was found, and his faithful dog sitting by it. A part of the body was eaten, but whether hunger had compelled the dog to the deed is not known'.[222] The man's name was Charles Gough. Mr de Quincey tells his history in Tait's Edinburgh Magazine [September 1839], together with the details of the accident, as called to mind by his ampler narrative of the fate of George and Sarah Green, two peasants of Easedale, who perished in the snow, as they were returning home across Langdale Fells, in the winter of 1807, leaving a family of six children, in whose favour Mr Wordsworth and his sister greatly interested themselves. The latter wrote a memorial of the calamity, which obtained pecuniary contributions for the orphans, from the royal family; and the former

---

[219] de Selincourt (III, 451) notes Field's letter mentioning Lamb's criticism (see Appendix).

[220] de Selincourt (III, 466) notes a letter from Field on 15 September 1837 making this suggestion.

[221] 'The Praise of Pindar', st. 3, *Poems*, Vol. I, p. 179. The punning underlining of *words worth* seems to be Field's.

[222] Anecdotes of the Life of Bishop Watson, 4to, p. 440 [BF].

composed the following stanzas on the event, which are not included in his published poems [IV, 375-6].[223]

[I think the last stanza of the poem entitled 'St Bees' [IV, 25] so obscure and unsatisfactory, that it would conclude better with the penultimate. And I would make the same observation as to 'Cora Linn' [III, 100], on account of the feebleness of the first couplet of its last stanza.]

In the thirteenth Sonnet during a Tour in Scotland in 1833, the poet did me the honour to shorten one needless Alexandrine [l. 12, IV, 31] at my suggestion;[224] but I think I observe, in the forty-third poem of Sentiment and Reflection ['The Warning', IV, 110], one or two others, which are not warranted by the sententiousness of the line, but *quas incuria fudit*. In philosophical poems, like 'The Happy Warrior' [IV, 86] and 'The Warning', an occasional weighty Alexandrine tones in well: e.g.

What knowledge can perform, is diligent to learn,

['Warrior', l. 9]

or

Past, future, shrinking up beneath th' incumbent *Now*.

['Warning', l. 96]

But of the following two I cannot see the necessity:

1. For the unconscious Babe an unbelated love, ['Warning', l. 29 (1837)[225]] and there is an apparent antithesis or synthesis—a clash— between the two *uns*, which is not intended. I suppose, as Crambo says, in Martinus Scriblerus, it was the poet's day for *uns*.

2. Of good or bad, whate'er be sought for or profess'd. 'Warning' [l. 90]. The sentiment in this passage reminds me of the following in Clarendon's History:— 'The Earl of Manchester thought all means lawful to compass that which is necessary, if the ways are unlawful which are proposed to bring it to pass'.

After all the winnowing and purging, and altering and restoring, that Mr Wordsworth's poems have received for thirty years, only three have been finally discarded from the collection, and left for execution, namely 'The Convict' [I, 312], 'The Glow-worm' [II, 466] and 'Andrew Jones' [II, 463]; and, like Mr Coleridge's friend, the

[223] Cp. Moorman, *Later Years*, pp. 127-30, where the 'memorial' is ascribed to Wordsworth and there is no mention of the royal family. Field apparently took these details as well as his text of the poem from De Quincey's article; see *Works*, Vol. XIII, pp. 126 and n., 146-7.
[224] de Selincourt (IV, 404) notes Field's letter of 17 December 1836.
[225] '. . . so prompt a love', 1843.

protector of 'Alice Fell',[226] I cannot agree with Mr Wordsworth as to the last of the three and take the liberty of reprieving him from the gallows . . .

In the thirty-fourth Sonnet during the Tour in Scotland of 1833 [IV, 44], Mr Wordsworth has adopted the line of Young,

> Whose merchants princes were, whose decks were thrones,

of which Dr Johnson says, 'Let burlesque try to go beyond this'.[227] I do not agree with him.

In illustration of the poem of the 'Old Cumberland Beggar' [IV, 234], I cannot deny myself the pleasure of quoting the following passage from one of Tieck's novels . . .[228] [Let it not be said that to give alms is to create mendicants. The poet himself pointed out to me the fine answer of the Spanish bishop to Mr Townsend the traveller, who asked him whether he did not think he was doing harm by so great a distribution of alms. 'Most undoubtedly', said he, 'but then it is the duty of the magistrate to clear the streets of beggars; it is my duty to give alms to all that ask'.][229]

In a note upon the Epitaph on Charles Lamb . . . Mr Wordsworth says—'This way of indicating the name of my lamented friend . . . a pilgrimage'. [ll. 23-4, IV, 272, and 1837 n., IV, 459]

I am sufficient lover of our old English literature, to think these playings with words graceful and beautiful, when the names are simple, and the double sense obvious. As long ago as when on my first Circuit, I transcribed the following from the monument in Hereford Cathedral, upon the Bishop of my name, who flourished there two hundred years since:—

> The Sunne that light unto three churches gave
> Is set. The Field is buried in a grave.
> This Sunne shall rise, this Field renew his flowers,
> That sweetness breathe for ages, not for hours.

[So Fuller calls the Bishop's greater contemporary, Dr Field, the author of the Book of the Church, 'that learned divine, whose memory

[226] *Biog. Lit.*, Vol. I, p. 54.

[227] 'Her merchants Princes, every deck a throne', 'The Merchant', II, st. 3, *Complete Works*, ed. John Doran, 2 vols, London 1854, Vol. II, p. 10; *Lives*, Vol. III, p. 398. Parallel not noted in de Selincourt.

[228] Lewis Tieck, *The Pictures* (*Die Gemälde*), tr. London 1825, pp. 80-1. The anecdote is of an old beggar who when he did not receive his accustomed alms from some villagers warned them that he might not come again: 'the man who is fortunate enough to be able to bestow receives more than the poor taker. . . . we are all brethren.'

[229] Joseph Townsend, *Journey Through Spain*, London 1791.

swelleth like a Field which the Lord hath blessed'. The following resembles the Epitaph alluded to by Mr Wordsworth [on Palmer, in his note on his lines on Lamb]:

> Palmers all my fathers were;
>   Palmer I lie buried here.
> I journey'd on, till worn with age,
> I quitted the world's pilgrimage,
>   On the blest Ascension-day,
>   In the cheerful month of May.

The following is from Fuller's Abel Redivivus, on Bp Jewell.

> Weight of courage[230] in Truth's duel
> Are the stones that make this Jewell:
>   Let him that would be truly blest
>   Wear this Jewell in his breast.]

Mr Wordsworth's five volumes of miscellaneous poems are appropriately concluded by the Ode, entitled 'Intimations of Immortality from recollections of early childhood', to which the opening lines of the volumes,

> The Child is Father of the Man, &c.

are affixed as a motto. The following little-known poem of the seventeenth century, by Henry Vaughan appears to me to involve the same sublime idea . . .[231] Charles Lamb would have liked this old poem. I wish I had lighted upon it before he died.

In the fourth book of the Excursion, is the following glorious passage, with the preceding germs of which in other poets I shall conclude this long Chapter:—

> Once more to distant ages of the world
> Let us revert . . .
>   [the Herdsman's] Fancy fetch'd,
> Ev'n from the blazing Chariot of the Sun,
> A beardless Youth, who touch'd a golden lute,
> And fill'd the illumin'd groves with ravishment.
> The nightly Hunter . . .
>   Or Pan himself,
> The simple Shepherd's awe-inspiring god.

>   [Bk IV, ll. 847-87, V, 135-7]

---

[230] This fact is questionable in Bishop Jewell. He had not the courage to give his body to be burned for his 'Apology' [BF].

[231] 'The Retreat', *Works*, ed. L. C. Martin, 2nd edn, Oxford 1957, pp. 419-20. Field was probably the first to draw attention to the comparison.

What Mr Wordsworth refers to the poetical Greeks, Boileau inculcates upon epic poetry.

> Là, pour nous enchanter, tout est mis en usage;
> Tout prends un corps, une âme, un esprit, un visage . . .[232]

And Mr Coleridge, in his translation of Wallenstein, ascribes to Love.

> For Fable is Love's world, his home, his birth-place . . .
> The intelligible forms of antient poets,
> The fair humanities of old religion,
> The power, the beauty, and the majesty,
> That had their haunts in dale, or piny mountain,
> Or forest by slow stream or pebbly spring,
> Or chasms and watry depths, all these have vanish'd.
> They live no longer in the faith of reason!
> But still the heart doth need a language; still
> Doth the old instinct bring back the old names . . .[233]

CHAPTER XI   The grand result of Mr Wordsworth's studies and meditations is the human and philosophic poem in blank verse entitled ī Excursion,—like the Faëry Queen, a portion only of a great sc e; but in itself independant, and, in my opinion, and what is of mucn more importance, in the growing opinion of the public, the noblest poetical work, that has appeared since the Paradise Regained of Milton.

[I name this name with all due reverence; but I am persuaded that Posterity will bear me out in the comparison. The biographer of Sir David Wilkie, a painter, for the most and best part, of humble life, has not feared to compare his subject with Raffaelle;[234] and there are many points of resemblance between Wordsworth and Wilkie. They both began their career with Rural Ballads and Village Politicians: truth to rustic feeling was their common magic: they were both looked down upon at first by academicians and critics: they both proceeded to subjects of Spanish liberty and independance: Peter Bell and the Waggoner may find parallels in the Peep of Day Boy and the Greenwich Pensioners: the Ecclesiastical Sonnets may compare with Wilkie's subjects from John Knox: and though Wordsworth never went to the East, like Wilkie, we have seen by one of his Letters that

---

[232] *Ars Poetique*, Chant III, ll. 163-72.
[233] This last parallel passage was first pointed out in Blackwood's Magazine, in the year 1823 [BF]. *The Piccolomini*, II, iv, 119-38, *Poems*, Vol. II, pp. 648-9.
[234] Cunningham's Life of Wilkie, Vol. III [London 1843, pp. 511-12] [BF].

he desired to write an oriental poem;[235] and his Ruth and Complaint
of an Indian Woman may teach us how well he would have succeeded.
To end our analogy, both these great Artists were patronized by that
true Mæcenas of his time, the late Sir George Beaumont; and each
finished his career as respectively Poet Laureate and Royal Limner.[236]
But here the comparison must stop. Wilkie could paint no pendant to
the Excursion, a poem which lifts its author, above not only the region
of Wilkie, but of Raffaelle himself, and warrants our placing our great
Poet in the sphere of Milton and Michael Angelo.]

The Excursion is the second part of a poem in three parts, intended
to be entitled The Recluse. In his preface, the author 'candidly
acknowledges that if the first of these had been completed, and in such
a manner as to satisfy his own mind, he should have preferred the
natural order of publication, and have given that to the world first. . . .
the two works have the same kind of relation to each other, if the
author may so express himself, as the ante-chapel has to the body of a
gothic church' [V, 1-2].

Shall we ever be permitted to enter this ante-chapel? We should
there read the best biography of the educational years of the poet.[237]
The friend, to whom Mr Wordsworth alludes, is Mr Coleridge, who,
'on the night after the former's recitation of his poem on the growth
of an individual mind', addressed the poet as follows . . .[238] If the ante-
chapel could be commemorated in such strains as these, surely the
body of the cathedral is not over-estimated by a reference to the lofty
edifices of Milton.

I am not insensible to the merits of Thomson, and Cowper, and
Burns, and feel that their contemporary[239] popularity forms exceptions

[235] *Letters, Later Years*, I, 340-1 (quoted in Field's third chapter).
[236] Beaumont died in 1827. Wordsworth accepted the Laureateship in 1843.
Wilkie, who died in 1840, was made Principal Painter in Ordinary in 1830.
[237] There are four extracts from this poem in the printed collection, viz. the
pieces entitled on the 'Influence of Natural Objects', 'There Was a Boy', the
'French Revolution', and the conclusion of the Postscript to the whole
collection [I, 248, II, 206, 264, 461] [BF].
[238] Field here quotes ll. 1-47 of 'To William Wordsworth . . .', *Poems*, Vol. I,
p. 403.
[239] It appears from the following testimonies that even these three poets had to
perform some quarantine. The observation of Thomson's biographer, quoted
by Mr Wordsworth in his Supplementary Essay, is not true ['"It was no
sooner read . . . than universally admired . . ."', II, 419]. 'When Thomson
published his "Winter", 1726, ⟨says Dr Warton⟩ it lay a long time neglected,
till Mr Spence made honorable mention of it, in his essay on the Odyssey,
which becoming a popular book, made the poem universally known.' 'The
immediate success of Cowper's first volume ⟨says Mr Hayley⟩ was very far
from being equal to its extraordinary merit. For some time it seemed to be

to the truth of Mr Wordsworth's doctrine, that 'every author as far
as he is great, and at the same time original, has had the task of creating
the taste, by which he is to be enjoyed; * * * * that in everything, which
is to send the soul into herself . . . the poet must reconcile himself for a
season to few and scattered hearers.' [Essay Supplementary, II, 426
('every . . . enjoyed') and 429] And if Mr Wordsworth had said 'for
ever', he would have been borne out by all the four great poets of our
language. Is either [*sic*] of these now read by any other than the few
and scattered? Shakspeare is occasionally recited upon the stage; but
by how many is he read, except perhaps for the story? 'Our wives'
certainly do not 'read Milton' now, whatever they may have done in
Pope's days; and Chaucer and Spenser are perused only by poetical
students.[240] When they wrote, the people can hardly be said to have
been readers at all; but the author of the 'Purple Island' (a contemporary
poem) says of Spenser, that he was, in his lifetime,

Discourag'd, scorn'd, his writings vilified;[241]

---

neglected by the public.' 'Only one edition of Burns's poems save the original
Kilmarnock one ⟨says the Literary Gazette of 13th February, 1841⟩ appeared
during the poet's life-time; yet he lived more than ten years after the publication by Geech which was in 1786, and was kept before the world by the
successive publication of his inimitable songs, in the musical collections of
Johnson and Thomson.' [BF]. Added later.

[240] Upon looking back into periodical criticism, I find these opinions confirmed
not only by Mr Henry Taylor, in a recent number of the Quarterly Review,
but in an excellent 'Portrait of Mr Wordsworth', written as long ago as the
year 1814, in the 'Champion' weekly paper, by my early friend and fellow-
student, the late Mr Thomas Barnes of 'the Times'—of which the following is
the conclusion:— 'Mr Wordsworth is not indeed adapted to be a popular
poet: he is of too high an order; he writes for men who reflect as deeply as
himself. Our greatest poets have not been popular: Shakspeare, notwithstanding his infinite variety, is rather liked, as affording scope to favorite
actors, than read in the closet: those who read him do it through the medium
of Cibber or Tate, or some other blundering fellow, who presumes to alter
and fit him for representation. As to Milton and Spenser, they are wholly unknown except to a few poetical readers: every library, indeed holds their works,
and most gentlemen are acquainted with their names; but you might travel
from Cornwall to Berwick, and not find twenty persons, who have fairly
perused Spenser's Fairy Queen, or even the Paradise Lost. Mr Wordsworth,
therefore, must be content to be less read than the writer of amorous odes and
wonderous romances: he may however be assured of an eternal memory in
the minds of the wise; and that future ages will be eager to point out his name,
as one of the proudest specimens of the best English character, distinguished,
as it will be, for purity of feeling, for comprehensiveness of intellect, and for a
strain of poetry, which at once enchants the senses, exalts the understanding,
and improves the heart' [BF]. Added later.

[241] *The Purple Island*, Canto I, st. 19, *Poetical Works of Giles and Phineas Fletcher*,
2 vols, Cambridge 1908-9, Vol. II, p. 16.

and Mr Wordworth has proved in this his Essay, that Shakspeare and Milton were not popular poets while they lived, though the people had then begun to read.

'It is certainly to be lamented ⟨says Pope himself⟩ that if any man does but endeavour to distinguish himself, or gratify others, by his studies, he is immediately treated as a common enemy, instead of being looked upon as a common friend; and assaulted as generally as if his whole design were to prejudice the state, or ruin the public. I will venture to say, no man ever rose to any degree of perfection in writing, but through obstinacy, and an inveterate resolution against the stream of mankind.' . . .[242]

It is the same in literary reform as with all moral and political improvement. The progression of the human race (observes Miss Martineau) must be carried on through persecution of some kind and degree, as it is clear that the superior spirits, to whom the race owes its advancement, must by their very act of anticipation get out of the circle of general intelligence and sympathy, and be thus subject to the trials of spiritual solitude and social enmity.[243] Thus has it ever been, and thus, by the laws of human nature, it must ever be. And so I say it is with the great leaders and reformers in the fine arts.

Our poet addresses Mr Haydon the painter thus:—

> High is our calling, Friend! Creative art . . .
> Great is the glory, for the strife is hard.

[III, 21]

['Il ne faut jamais juger d'une pièce par les succès des premières années: le temps seul met le prix aux ouvrages; et l'opinion réfléchie des bons uges est, à la longue, l'arbitre du public'.[244] And yet, in the teeth of all these authorities, Mr Jeffrey, in the Edinburgh Review, used always to be contending that it was the duty of criticism to follow, and not to lead, public opinion, and that the poet should cultivate present popularity, which was generally an earnest of future fame. 'While we ⟨he grandiloquently says, in one place[245]⟩ who profess the stately

---

[242] Field has here a string of similar passages, some added later, to the effect that the poet and his age are enemies and he must stamp his character on the age rather than be stamped by it. Field quotes from Diderot, Corneille, Dugald Stewart, Schiller and A. W. von Schlegel, commenting 'all the great German writers hold the same opinions'. I have not traced Pope's remark.

[243] Field may be referring to *Society in America*, 3 vols, London 1837, from which he quotes below.

[244] Voltaire [BF].

[245] Edinb. Rev. Vol. xvii, p. 430, et seq. [BF]. The paragraphs quoted are from the review of Southey's *Curse of Kehama*.

office of correcting and instructing, are yet willing in most things, to bow to the authority of public judgment, we really cannot help thinking that a poet, whose sole object is to give delight and to gain glory, ought to show something of the same docility. ... But the cases, we believe, are wonderfully rare in which that mysterious and inacessessible Judge [Posterity] has ever reversed the unfavorable sentences of the ordinary jurisdictions. ... Mr Scott has ... imparted a spirit, a force and variety to his pictures, by keeping his readers perpetually engaged with events and persons, that bear a character of historical importance, instead of soothing them, like the author before us [Southey], with the virtues and affections, as well as the marvels and legends, of the nursery.' Is it surprising that such a public demand as this created the supply of verse, which Mr Southey himself most appropriately termed the Satanic School of poetry?] We of this generation know very well who were the popular poets during all the time that Mr Wordsworth was slowly creating the taste by which he was to be relished, namely Sir Walter Scott and Lord Byron. Of the former I shall say little [since he always reverenced the lyre of Wordsworth and knew that his own poetical romances were inferior to Mr Southey's]; but I will quote a passage from the Preface to the tragedy of 'Philip Van Artevelde' which appears to me to be conclusive of the unconscious doom of the scornful latter: 'There is no such thing ⟨says Mr Henry Taylor⟩ as philosophical misanthropy ... it will never, in the long run of time, approve itself equal to the institution of a poetical fame of the highest and most durable order.'[246]

'The idea of happiness ⟨justly observes the poet Campbell⟩ is the sovereign feeling of poetry. It lurks even in poetic misanthropy, when she tries to shape an infernal paradise out of her own pride and independance.' [That ⟨as Cowley says⟩ is but

> dull and earthy poesy,
> Where grief and misery can be joined with verse.[247]]

Let us test this.

> There is a calm for those who weep ...
> Nor leave one wretched trace behind
> Resembling me.

Lord Byron doubtless thought the above stanzas by Montgomery a perfect poem. Indeed he has imitated their measure in the last verses he

[246] *Works*, 5 vols, London 1877-8, Vol. I, pp. x-xi.
[247] 'On the Death of Mr William Hervey', st. 19, *Poems*, Vol. I, p. 37.

ever wrote; for (original as he could occasionally be) he was also a great imitator, among others, of Wordsworth himself. The stanzas are such as his lordship would and could have written. Now hear how the true poet, Mr Montgomery, goes on to moralize and sweeten the strain:—

. . .

The Soul, immortal as its Sire,
Shall never die![248]

This is one of the poems, specially instanced, of which the Edinburgh Review says:— 'There is a certain cold extravagance, which is symptomatic of extreme dullness; and wild metaphors, and startling personifications, indicate the natural sterility of the mind, which has been forced to bear them'. From such a critique, Mr Montgomery's poems were generously vindicated by Mr Southey, in the Quarterly Review.[249]

Göethe's judgment of Lord Byron is to the same effect as Mr Henry Taylor's. He reproaches the noble poet with the negative, the gloomy tendency of his mind. . . . He calls such works 'the literature of Despair'.

Mr Hazlitt has not, in his 'Spirit of the Age', expressly condemned Lord Byron on this, the true ground. . . . 'It has been asked ⟨he says⟩ whether Lord Byron is a writer likely to live? perhaps not: he has intensity of power, but wants distinctive character. In my opinion, Mr Wordsworth is the only poet of the present day, that is likely to live—should he ever be born! But who will be the midwife to bring his works to light? It is a question whether Milton would have been popular without the help of Addison; nay, it is a question whether he is so, even with it.'[250]

Occulta veritas tempore patet. Time, the great midwife, has, since this was written [1823], brought Mr Wordsworth's works to light. Again, in his Lectures on the Poets, Mr Hazlitt writes:— 'The Giaour, the Corsair, Childe Harold, are all the same person, and they are apparently all himself . . . [Byron's single mind] is like a cancer eating into the heart of poetry. But still there is power, and power rivets attention, and forces admiration. He hath a dæmon; and that is the next thing to being full of the god'.[251]

---

[248] 'The Grave', sts 1-5, 6-30, *Poetical Works*, Vol. I, 55-60; Byron, 'On This Day I Complete My Thirty-Sixth Year', *Poetical Works*, ed. E. H. Coleridge, London 1905, p. 1040.
[249] Edinburgh Review, vol. ix p. 351 [BF]. *Quarterly Review*, Vol. VI, pp. 405 ff.
[250] *Complete Works*, Vol. XI, pp. 69-78 and (quoted) Vol. XX, p. 128.
[251] *Complete Works*, Vol. V, p. 153.

To be a great poet (as Cicero says of being a good orator) it is necessary to be a good man[252]:—

> Nec sponsæ laqueum famoso carmine nectit.
> —Horatius.

It is necessary to have faith in goodness. Nothing sublime can be written or done without this. Lord Byron had faith only in evil; and that is the secret of his power in the gloomy and terrible of poetry. He *saw* only the dark clouds before the sun; but he should have trusted that this was not all—

> nor have the clouds
> Only one face, but on the side of heaven,
> Keep ever gorgeous beds of golden light.
> —Leigh Hunt.

[There is a fine speech to this effect from the mouth of Beethoven, recorded in Göethe's Correspondence with a Child: 'Music, like her sister arts, is based upon morality—that fountain-head of genuine invention! . . . Man's aim is fixed by the same hand from above which helps him to attain it.']

Mr Southey and Mr Crabbe, poets of greater originality than Lord Byron, were never popular;[253] but their fame will increase, while that

---

[252] 'For if men will impartially and not asquint, look towards the offices and functions of a poet, they will easily conclude to themselves the impossibility of any man's being a good poet without first being a good man.'—Ben Jonson, *Pref. to the Fox* [BF].

[253] Five and twenty years ago, the most generous of publishers [my late friend John Murray] [*d.* 1843] gave Mr Crabbe three thousand pounds for his Tales of the Hall; but I question whether he ever reimbursed himself. Mr Moore is also said to have received the like sum from the house of Longman & Co. for Lalla Rookh. Such copy-money can never be given again; for the day of two guinea quartos is gone by. Books must now be cheap and of many copies, not dear and of few. Even 'a lord's happy lines' could scarcely command such sums again, as Mr Murray paid to Lord Byron. Sir Walter Scott's enormous copy-sales would form no precedent, supposing equal genius to occur; for in consequence of his unfortunate partnership with his printer and of the failure of his principal publisher, the prices were little better than nominal. Novels are the only books that keep up their cost to the public, however their copy-rights may have fallen to their authors. The world 'says nothing to our paradoxes' and poetry nowadays. Nothing is read but novels and periodical publications, and even the novels are published periodically. Mr Southey could at any time have earned more money by writing *currente calamo* an article for the Quarterly Review, than by 'meditating the thankless Muse' in such a beautiful poem as the Tale of Paraguay [BF].

of Sir Walter Scott's poetry is already gone, and that of Lord Byron is fast decreasing. Mr Campbell and Mr Rogers (like Gray and Gold-smith) are elegant minor poets. Mr Bowles and Mr Montgomery (like Collins and the Wartons) are true lyricks. I consider Mr Moore (like Darwin) to be a very artificial poet. Lord Byron asserts that Shakspeare and Spenser were popular in their lifetimes, but admits that Milton was not. He adduces no proof for these assertions; and we read that he possessed no copy of Shakspeare, ranked both him and Milton below Pope; and 'could see nothing in Spenser'.[254] His notions of the supremacy of Pope are quite a superstition, as if to imitate Pope would make a greater poet than to be original. He says:— 'The disciples of Pope were Johnson, Goldsmith, Rogers, Campbell, Crabbe, Gifford, Mathias, Hayley and the author of the Paradise of Coquettes, to whom may be added Richards, Heber, Wrangham, Bland, Hodgson, Merivale and others, who have not had their full fame, because the race is not always to the swift, nor the battle to the strong, and because there is a fortune in fame, as in all other things. [****] Now it is remarkable ⟨he adds⟩ that all the followers of Pope, whom I have named, have produced beautiful and standard works, and it was not the number of his imitators who finally hurt his fame, but the despair of imitation, and the ease of not imitating him sufficiently'.[255]

Mr Southey and Mr Montgomery, critics and poets both, are of a directly contrary opinion to Lord Byron.

'Of all the poets, in the intermediate half century before Cowper ⟨says Mr Southey, in his interesting life of that poet⟩ not one who attained to any distinction, which he has since held, or is likely to hold, was of the school of Pope. That school has produced versifiers in abundance, but no poet. No man of genius nor even of original talents, acknowledged his supremacy, while his authority was paramount with the public and its blind guides.'[256]

'It is to be remarked ⟨says Mr Montgomery, in his admirable Lectures⟩ that though Pope gave the tone, character and fashion to the verse of his day . . . yet of all his imitators not one has maintained the rank of even a second-rate author. . . . It is only when mannerism is connected with genius of the proudest order, or the most prolific species, that it becomes extensively infectious among minor minds. . . . [Goldsmith and Churchill] are remembered and admired for what they possessed independent of him, each having wealth enough of his own

[254] Hunt's Lord Byron, 8vo, vol. i p. 77 [BF].
[255] Moore's Lord Byron, 8vo, vol. iii, pp. 59, 60 [BF].
[256] Cowper, *Works*, Vol. II, p. 142-3.

to be a freeholder of Parnassus, after paying off any mortgage on his little estate, due to that enormous capitalist.'[257]

Churchill was a decided follower of Dryden, and, as such, a favorite with Cowper, who disliked Pope. Of the names enumerated by Lord Byron, Johnson was no poet; Goldsmith was no disciple of Pope; Rogers, Campbell and Crabbe owe little to Pope. Of the rest, Time has not confirmed the poetical character. It was Cowper that was the first reviver of natural poetry, and he expressly protests against Pope, as having

Made poetry a mere mechanic art.

Gray acknowledged himself a follower of Dryden. Collins, Thomson, Akenside, Armstrong, Beattie and Burns owed nothing to Pope. Southey, Wilson, Montgomery, Shelley, Keats, Procter, Lamb, Lloyd, Landor, Horace Smith, Leigh Hunt, Coleridge, Hartley Coleridge, Mrs Hemans, Talfourd, Trench, Allen Cunningham, Browning, Longfellow, Horne, Calder, Campbell, Milnes, Stirling, Reade, Kenyon, Harness, Moultric, Faber, owe their obligations to Wordsworth.[258]

Major a longinquo reverentia. Distance of place bears some analogy to length of time: the voice of another hemisphere is the prophecy of that of posterity. Miss Martineau says that in America, 'Byron is scarcely heard of: Wordsworth lies at the heart of the people. His name may not be so often spoken as some others; but I have little doubt that his influence is as powerful as that of any author. It is less diffused, but stronger. His works are not to be had at every store; but within people's houses, they lie under the pillow, or open on the work-box, or they peep out of the coat-pocket: they are marked, remarked and worn'.[259]

Lord Byron is equally an infidel to his own poetry, and expressly says that *he* has never contemplated the prospect of 'filling permanently a station in the literature of his country'. These (quoted in mockery) are Mr Wordsworth's just words of himself; and I think it may be much more clearly proved that no poet was ever immortal, who had not faith in his own powers, and did not believe and even prophesy,

---

[257] 'A View of Modern English Literature: I', *Lectures*, pp. 365-6.
[258] It is curious that since these Memoirs were written, not one of the οἱ πολλοί enumerated by Lord Byron, and most of the last-mentioned names, are included by Mr Hall, in his Gems of Modern Poets [*The Book of Gems*, ed. S. C. Hall, 3 vols, London 1836-8] [BF].
[259] Harriet Martineau, *Society in America*, Vol. III, p. 219.

that he should be so, than that no great poet is popular in his life-time . . .[260]

[The difference between poetry of the school of Wordsworth and of that of Pope may be well illustrated by a comparison of their own descriptions of their respective summer-houses. Mr Wordsworth's was an Out-house on the Island of Grasmere.

> Thou seest a homely Pile; yet to these walls
> The heifer comes in the snow-storm . . .
> Creations lovely as the work of sleep—
> Fair sights and visions of romantic joy!

['Written . . . on the Island at Grasmere', ll. 14-30, IV, 198]

Pope describes his grotto at Twickenham as follows:— 'From the river Thames, you see through my arch up a walk of the wilderness, to a kind of open Temple. . . . When you shut the doors of this grotto, it becomes on the instant, from a luminous room, a *camera obscura*. . . . The bottom is paved with simple pebble, as is also the adjoining walk up the wilderness to the temple, in the natural taste, agreeing not ill with the little dripping murmur, and the aquatic idea of the whole place'.[261]

> I mused; and, thirsting for redress,
> Recoil'd into the wilderness.

['Effusion . . . near Dunkeld', ll. 127-8, III, 105]

CHAPTER XII   The high argument of all Mr Wordsworth's poems is that—not in the metaphysical sense of either material or essential ubiquity, but in a more poetical sense—

Jupiter est quod eumque vides, quocumque moveris.[262]

---

[260] Field is referring to Byron's unpublished reply (given in part by Moore) to an article in *Blackwood's Edinburgh Magazine*; see *Works*, ed. R. E. Prothero, 6 vols, London 1900, Vol. IV, p. 488. Wordsworth's words are in the Preface to *Peter Bell*, II, 331. Field continues by commenting again on Byron and Scott and then gives a handful of quotations about artistic purity, fame and the difficulty of discussing poetry 'in any other than its own divine dialect'. He remarks that Thomson and Burns owed something of their immediate celebrity to their nationality and Cowper something to Calvinistic sectarianism.

[261] *Correspondence*, ed. George Sherburn, 5 vols, Oxford 1956, Vol. II, pp. 296-7.

[262] Lucanus [BF].

> The Being that is in the clouds and air,
> That is in the green leaves among the groves.
>
> ['Hart-Leap Well', ll. 165-6, II, 254]

And it has been expressly allowed to poets to

> look thro' Nature up to Nature's God—
> Pursue that chain, which links th' immense design, . . .
> And know where faith, law, morals, all began,
> All end, in love of God and love of Man.[263]

Mr Wordsworth's poetical religion does not differ from that of the most pious and beautiful of modern religious poets.

> The Lord of all, himself thro' all diffus'd,
> Sustains and is the life of all that lives. . . .
> But all are under One.[264]

That is the scriptural doctrine. The other is polytheism; but the phrases, 'himself thro' all diffus'd—'is the life'—, are more like pantheism or Spinozism, than any passage in Mr Wordsworth; and yet Mr Coleridge, who has elsewhere done ample justice to his great brother-poet, in a late indiscreetly-published Letter, says that 'the vague, misty (rather than mysterious) confusion of God with the world, and the accompanying Nature-worship, is the trait in his poetic works, which he most dislikes as unhealthful, and denounces as contagious'.[265] The same writer, in his 'Aids to Reflection', has expressly acquitted Mr Wordsworth's language of 'the sense or purpose of Nature worship',[266] and there is no doubt that the Excursion is no more pantheistic than the Task. It appears to me that, without Christianity such poetry as Mr Wordsworth's would never have existed. The polytheistic Greeks made gods of the works of Nature; but they had no more descriptive poetry than they had landscape-painting. Their idolatry was the antithesis of such Nature-worship as Mr Wordsworth's—else some poet would have arisen among them like Shakspeare, Spenser or Milton (in their descriptive passages), Akenside, Thomson, Cowper or Wordsworth. 'Descriptions of rural objects in the antient writers ⟨says Mr Twining⟩ are almost always what may be called *sensual* descriptions. They describe them not as beautiful, but as pleasant, as pleasures not of

---

[263] *Essay on Man*, Bk IV, ll. 332-40, *Poetical Works*, p. 277.
[264] *The Task*, Bk VI, ll. 221-38, *Poetical Works*, pp. 224-5.
[265] *Letters*, Vol. V, pp. 94-5. Field has referred to this letter earlier; see n. 60.
[266] *Aids to Reflection*, London 1884 (Bohn edn), p. 271. Field is using the 1825 edn, and alters the wording slightly.

the imagination, but of the external senses. Socrates said he could learn nothing from the fields and trees.'[267] Of Christian poets, 'the fields are the study—Nature is the book';[268] and they

> Find tongues in trees, books in the running brooks,
> Sermons in stones, and good in everything.

The Essay on Man was far more plausibly accused of Spinozism than the Excursion can be; yet Bishop Warburton succesfully defended Pope's poem from the attack of Monsieur de Crousaz, if he failed to prove the Christianity of the poem.

A very different view from that of Mr Coleridge, was taken of this trait in Mr Wordsworth's poetry, by a professedly religious periodical publication (the Eclectic Review), on the first appearance of the Excursion:—

'In this great work ⟨says the eloquent writer, perhaps the Revd John Foster⟩ . . . the principles and evidence of the author's system of ethics are splendidly, if not clearly and fully, unfolded. . . . By this blissful converse of the human soul with the "soul of things", the former grows wiser and better of necessity, while it spontaneously surrenders itself to the moralizing influence of all external circumstances, "working together for good" . . .'[269]

This is the Platonic procession to the love of God from the love of Nature and of Man—from the love of the beautiful and the good to that of Him who is all beauty and goodness. The converse doctrine—'the high *priori* road'[270]—is doubtless the more noble; but I see no confusion, or stopping at Nature-worship, in the poet's system. Barrow, in his immortal sermon on Divine Love, arrives at the same blessed effects, proceeding downwards from the love of God to the love of Man . . .[271]

Our poet expressly speaks of himself, in one place, as

> chang'd from what I was, when first
> I came among these hills . . .

['Tintern Abbey', ll. 66-111, II, 261-2]

[267] Twining's Aristotle, p. 230 [BF].
[268] Bloomfield [BF]. 'The Farmer's Boy: Spring', l. 32, *Poetical Works*, London 1864, p. 18.
[269] Eclectic Review for January, 1815 [BF]. The passage ends with a quotation from *The Excursion*, Bk IV, ll. 1270-5, V, 149.
[270] Pope [BF]. *The Dunciad*, Bk IV, l. 471, *Poetical Works*, p. 574.
[271] Field here quotes from what is apparently a version of the second sermon on Charity; see *Works*, ed. A. Napier, 9 vols, Cambridge 1859, Vol. II, pp. 280-2 (Sect. VI).

Surely such a worshipper of Nature as this is 'not far from the kingdom of God'[272] ...

This last passage ['Immortality Ode', st. XI] leads me to point out the real peculiarity of Mr Wordsworth's poetical theory, which is the notion of universal sensibility, like the philosophical dogma of Thomas Campanella, an Italian writer of the early part of the seventeenth century. 'All things ⟨he says⟩ feel; else would the world be a chaos ...'

> Each leaf, that and this, his neighbour will kiss,
> Each wave, one and t'other, speeds after his brother.

['Stray Pleasures', ll. 34-5, II, 161]

'Contrariety ⟨he adds⟩ is necessary for the decay and reproduction of Nature; but all things strive against their contraries, which they could not do, if they did not perceive what is their contrary.' 'They might ⟨said Trim⟩ if it had pleased God.' 'God ⟨continues Campanella⟩ ... said, let all things feel, some more, some less, as they have more or less necessity to imitate my being.'[273] And so says the creative Poet of his

---

[272] Mark, xii, 34 [BF]. Field also quotes a line from Daniel, 'Neighb'ring on Heaven, and that no foreign land'. On Wordsworth's poetry he then quotes 'A Poet's Epitaph', ll. 51-2, 45-8, IV, 67; 'Song at the Feast of Brougham Castle', ll. 161-4, II, 258; 'Hart-Leap Well', ll. 97-100, II, 252; and 'Peter Bell', ll. 131-45, II, 336-7. On what 'Wordsworth's system is to teach us' Field quotes 'At the Grave of Burns, 1803', ll. 35-6, II, 66; *The Excursion*, Bk III, ll. 231-2, V, 821; 'Lines ... Yew-Tree', ll. 50-64, I, 94; 'Personal Talk', ll. 27-8, IV, 74; 'Peter Bell', ll. 248-50, 1072, II, 341, 380; 'The Old Cumberland Beggar', ll. 147-53, IV, 239; 'To the Same [Lycoris]', ll. 12-13, IV, 96; and the 'Immortality Ode', st. 11, IV, 285. He comments, 'There is a cluster of grapes for the reader, on his entrance into the vineyard of Rydal Mount'. To 'Peter Bell', ll. 248-50 ('A primrose, by a river's brim ...') Field has two notes, added at different times: 'The whole scope of my poetry (said Mr W. to me one day) is to teach mankind that a primrose is something more than a primrose'; and a long note about the article in *Blackwood's Magazine* in March 1841 which argued that this and the four following stanzas serve merely to 'associate with an object, which itself affords no poetry, some other which does, and then, under pretence of describing the first, do little in reality but describe the second. ... There are lines present every one hastens to pluck from the poem ... as the utterance of the poet.' Field argues interestingly that Peter Bell is not 'unpoetic', but in order to show how 'sympathy with affliction can change even a heart of stone into one of flesh', it was necessary first to show 'the original obtuseness of the travelling potter'. He feels that 'this peasant has the relation of contrast to peasants in general, who are sensible, however silently, to the beauties of nature'—such as Akenside's swain, whose 'rude expression and untutor'd air, Beyond the power of language, will unfold The form of beauty smiling at his heart'. *Pleasures of Imagination* (1744), III, *Poetical Works*, p. 56.

[273] Hallam's History of Literature [*Literature of Europe*, 4 vols, London 1837-9], vol. iii, pp. 145, 146 [BF].

being. So too we read in the laws of Menu, that it is the creed of the Hindu, that vegetables, as well as animals, have internal consciousness, and are sensible of pleasure and pain.[274] It is Mr Wordsworth's poetical

> faith, that every flower
> Enjoys the air it breathes.

['Lines Written in Early Spring', ll. 11-12, IV, 58]

All this Nature-worship by no means supersedes revealed religion, as it is too apt to do, with some treatise-writers on natural theology, who mix up their own ingenious solutions with the problems of the Deity, and thus worship themselves.

> And if indeed there be
> An all-pervading Spirit, upon whom
> Our dark foundations rest, and He design
> That this magnificent effect of power,
> The earth we tread, the sky which we behold
> By day, and all the pomp which night reveals,
> That these, and that superior mystery,
> Our vital frame. . . .
> No more than as a mirror that reflects
> To proud Self-love her own intelligence?

[*The Excursion*, Bk IV, ll. 968-78, 989, 991-2, V, 139-40]

Mr Wordsworth's life is doubtless reflected in many particulars by that of the lowly-minded hero of his great poem; and of him it is said—

> What soul was his, when from the naked top,
> Of some bold headland, he beheld the sun
> Rise up and bathe the world in light! . . .
>   the least of things
> Seem'd infinite; and there his spirit shap'd
> Her prospects; nor did he believe;—he *saw*.

[*The Excursion*, Bk I, ll. 198-232 (203-5 om.), V, 15-16]

I have now quoted more than enough to send every reader, who is not already acquainted with the poetry of Wordsworth, to the study of his volumes. For himself,

> at so ripe an age
> As twice seven years[275]

[274] Field here notes Campanella's romance, *The City of the Sun*, in which the people concluded that 'ignoble things were created for the use of noble things, and then ate all things without scruple'. Hallam, Vol. III, p. 682.
[275] Cowper, *The Task*, Bk IV, ll. 713-14, *Poetical Works*, p. 197.

The Memoirs

in the year 1800,—well does he recollect where,—the writer of these
Memoirs first heard read—gratefully does he remember by whom—
the sweet poem entitled 'We are Seven'; and he has ever since been,
through evil report and through good report, an admirer (and subsequently a friend) of the poet. He has cheered the rugged paths of
professional studies with the Lyrical Ballads, and has carried the
Excursion round his forensic circuit, at the hazard of ridicule from the
whole Edinburgh-Review-blinded Bar.

> My shame in crowds, my solitary pride.
> —Goldsmith.

His readings met with somewhat greater respect from the fair daughters
of Sabrina and Vaga; but he could detect that even they preferred
Sir Walter Scott's storied minstrelsy, Lord Byron's dark tales, or
Mr Moore's artificial flowers, to Comus, the Antient Mariner or the
Lines on Tintern Abbey. Still even in those evil days, he had the good
fortune to make one convert to his poetical faith, in a young heart, who
is now deservedly the leader of that circuit, and author of the most
beautiful tragedy of our times, such as the poet of 'Laodamia' would
(if he could) have written.[276]

> Can haughty Time be just?
> ['Upon the Same Occasion', September 1819,
> l. 60, IV, 101]

It can.

> Now another day is come ...
> For everlasting blossoming.
> ['Song at the Feast of Brougham Castle',
> ll. 138-9, then 7-10, II, 258, 254]

The bar of the northern circuit, on one occasion, did themselves the
honour of rising, with a feeling between respect and curiosity (call it

[276] Field refers to Thomas Noon Talfourd, who in a later Preface to his tragedy
Ion, 1835, acknowledged this influence. Talfourd published two sympathetic
essays on Wordsworth and spoke warmly of him in introducing the Copyright Act (see Moorman, *Later Years*, pp. 321, 552-5; and nn. 5 and 33 above).
  Field later added this note: 'I cannot flatter myself that I had an equal share
in the conversion of my early friend Mr Leigh Hunt. He was my senior,
and it was my part, in general, to learn from him. But that conversion was so
compleat, that, whereas in the first edition of the Feast of the Poets in 1814,
only Campbell, Moore, Scott and Southey are entertained by Apollo, and
Wordsworth and Coleridge are turned out of the room, in the second, in
1815, the latter are not only feasted, but Wordsworth is made the King of
the whole.'

respect) upon Mr Wordsworth's entrance into Court;[277] and even
Mr Brougham, in adverting to him as a witness, uttered an un-
trembling belief in his immortal genius, which induces me to hope
that not he, as has been reported, but Mr Jeffrey again, was the author
of those fatal words, as applied to the Excursion—'*This will never do*'—
fatal not to the poet, but to the critic.[278] The poetical criticisms in the
Edinburgh Review rest now merely monuments of the tastelessness
and heartlessness of their author. Quam nihil (as the motto to the
second edition of the Lyrical Ballads said)

> Quam nihil ad genium, Papiniane, tuum!

and the curious reader of these articles, unborn at their first appearance,
wonders how there were any who could be influenced by such things;
but (as Sheridan replies, in his 'Critic'), the number of those, who
undergo the fatigue of judging for themselves, is very small indeed. In
the same Edinburgh Review that put forth, from time to time, Mr
Jeffrey's censures of Wordsworth, appeared the following passage from
the more temperate pen of the late Sir James McIntosh:— 'The failure
of innumerable adventurers is inevitable in literary, as well as in
political revolutions. The inventor seldom perfects his invention. . . .
[He is] supplanted in general estimation by more cautious and skilful
imitators.'

This fate has not befallen our great poetical revolutionist. . . . What
he began in the admiration of the few, and the ridicule of the many,
he has been permitted to live to perfect in almost universal love and
respect—his poetry will be for ever remembered—and, though it will
influence the genius of all his successors, yet it will be strange and
contrary to literary experience if imitation, however cautious and
skilful, shall supplant originality. Sir James proceeds:—
'. . . erroneous theories respecting poetical diction—exclusive and
proscriptive notions in criticism . . . and a neglect of that extreme
regard to general sympathy and even accidental prejudice . . . have

[277] Wordsworth and Southey were summoned as expert witnesses on the
genuineness of some letters in the famous Marsden will case in September
1836. See Moorman, *Later Years*, p. 544.

[278] A fatality, has in a great previous political instance, attended these words. It
was in answer to them, as used by the French royalists, at the Revolution, that
the tremendously popular song of *Ça ira* was composed. Prophets should be
more cautious of employing the phrase in future. However politically a
conservative, Mr Wordsworth is a poetical reformer; and the French political
revolution had more connection with this English poetical one than good
people would think. It is a curious coincidence to find the old poetical royalists
of the Edinburgh Review crying *Ça n'ira pas*, and the revolutionary public at
length receiving the new poet with *This will do*! [BF]

powerfully counteracted an attempt, equally moral and philosophical
... to enlarge the territories of art, by unfolding the poetical interest,
which lies latent in the common acts of humblest men, and in the most
ordinary modes of feeling, as well as in the most familiar scenes of
nature.'[279]

We are indebted to the Life of Sir James McIntosh, published in
1835, for his interesting Journal in India, where under date the 6th July
1808, he says of Mr Jeffrey's first article on Wordsworth, which we
examined in our fourth and ninth Chapters, that it is 'very unjust and
anti-poetical. I have just got, by a most lucky chance, Wordsworth's
new poems. I owe them some delightful hours of abstraction from the
petty vexations of the little world where I live, and the horrible
dangers of the great world, to which my feelings are attached. I applied
to him his own verses ['Personal Talk', ll. 51-3, IV, 75] ... The
Sonnets on Switzerland and Milton are sublime. Some of the others
are in a style of severe simplicity, sometimes bordering on the hardness
and dryness of some of Milton's sonnets. Perhaps it might please him
to know that his poetry has given these feelings to one at so vast a
distance; it is not worth adding, to one who formerly had foolish
prejudices against him'.

Most heartily does the present writer sympathize with these softened
feelings of long distant judicial banishment. 'A thousand leagues ⟨as
Dr Franklin says⟩ have nearly the same effect with a thousand years'.
Mr Jeffrey should have read Mr Wordsworth's new poems, not at the
Stove of the Outer House, but, as Sir James McIntosh and I did, in
another hemisphere, escaped from 'the drowsy bench, the wrangling
bar'.[280] *Et in Arcadia ego.* In the course of his personal communication
with Mr Wordsworth, which, from such foreign residence on his part
has been all too little, the present writer has frequently enjoyed the
charm of hearing the bard recite his own verses; and heartily therefore
can he apply to him his own language:

> I love to hear that eloquent old man
> Pour forth his meditations ...
>
> the various forms of things,
> Caught in their fairest, happiest attitude.

[*The Excursion*, Bk IX, ll. 459-64, V, 301]

This expression will remind the reader of Dr Akenside's Pleasures of
Imagination:—

[279] Edinburgh Review, vol. xxii, p. 38 [BF].
[280] Blackstone [BF].

and before him turn
The fairest, happiest, attitude of things[281]

and as both that poem and the Excursion profess to unfold

With what attractive charms, this goodly frame
Of Nature touches the consenting hearts
Of mortal men . . .[282]

and as this philosophy appears to resemble that of Mr Wordsworth's great poem, it becomes necessary to advert to the Pleasures of Imagination, another unfinished poem in blank verse [and which has also been unjustly accused of a want of religion]. Again Dr Akenside addresses 'some heavenly genius':—

Oh, teach me to reveal the grateful charm
That searchless Nature o'er the sense of man
Diffuses; to behold, in lifeless things,
The inexpressive semblance of himself,
Of thought and passion.

and adds in a note:— 'This similitude is the foundation of almost all the ornaments of poetic diction';[283] but by poetic diction, Dr Akenside means poetry here; so that we take nothing by that notion.

Not a breeze
Flies o'er the meadow, not a cloud imbibes
The setting sun's effulgence . . .
Thus the men,
Whom Nature's works can charm, with God himself
Hold converse; grow familiar, day by day,
With his conceptions; act upon his plan,
And form to his the relish of their souls.[284]

I consider, in spite of the cold opinions of Gray and Johnson, that this poem evinces the *mens divinior*; but the Excursion appears to me to be a work of a much higher order. The poet of Imagination perpetually cramps himself by didactics: the professor's square cap and gown are constantly obtruded. The subject is mere metaphysics poetically treated, and the poem wants not only the divineness but the humanity

---

[281] *Pleasures of Imagination* (1744), Book I, *Poetical Works*, p. 5.
[282] Ibid., Book I, p. 4 (first three lines). Field also quotes here, from Book I, 'But some to higher hopes . . . The transcript of Himself', p. 7, and 'The passions gently soothed away . . . As airs that fan the summer', pp. 7-8.
[283] Ibid., Book III, p. 50 and n.
[284] Ibid., Book III, pp. 58-9 (conclusion).

The Memoirs

of the more enlarged Excursion. Having suffered the author of the Pleasures of Imagination[285] to open his own theme, let us do equal justice to Mr Wordsworth:

> Of Truth, of Grandeur, Beauty, Love and Hope ...
> which they with blended might
> Accomplish:— this is our high argument.
>
> [*Prospectus to The Excursion*, ll. 14-71, V, 3-5]

Highly as it is praised by Dr Johnson and Mr Southey, the blank verse of Akenside is, in my humble opinion, inferior to this in grandeur and harmony. Much of Akenside's is as prosaic as a metaphysical treatise, which the whole poem too nearly resembles. I consider Mr Wordsworth's versification to be the most Miltonic since the Paradise Lost, with the latinity of the great epic poet properly exchanged, by our narrative and interlocutory moralist, for the happy simplicity of the dramatic Shakspeare. The quotations from Wordsworth, which are in everybody's mouth, taste more like Shakspeare than any other poet.

It is therefore not without sensibility to the philosophical poetry of Dr Akenside—to the awful but too paradoxical sententiousness of the Night Thoughts (Dr Young was the Pope of blank verse)—to the elegant descriptiveness of the Seasons;[286] and to the original eloquence of the Task (a happy union of Young and Thomson, in religious and descriptive poetry, but more natural than either) that I have ventured to pronounce Mr Wordsworth to be the greatest poet that has risen in England since the star of Milton 'dwelt apart', and to have fully redeemed his bold pledge of recording in verse a work, which, to use his own words,

> The high and tender Muses shall accept,
> With gracious smile, deliberately pleas'd,
> And listening Time reward with sacred praise.
>
> [*The Excursion*, Bk I, ll. 105-7, V, 11]

Finis.

---

[285] Field here has a long note suggesting a way of stitching together the best parts of the two versions of the poem, so that 'the dull and somewhat irrelevant episodes... (which Dr Johnson objects to) are omitted, and few or no beauties are sacrificed that are to be found in either version.'

[286] I should not have thought worth mentioning a sort of imitation of the poem by Mallet in two cantos, but for its title *The Excursion* [2 vols, 1728]. [BF] Mallet was a student with Thomson in Edinburgh.

APPENDIX No I *Extracts from the Reviews of the Lyrical Ballads.*
[Field quotes from the 'three principal reviews' of the first edition;
briefly from the 'dull' *Monthly Review*, XXIX, June 1799 and the
Critical Review, XXIV, October 1798, and more fully from the
'wonderfully liberal' notice in the 'Quarterly of its day—the high
church-and-king' *British Critic*, XIV, October 1799. He wishes to show
that Cottle's (or Wordsworth's) recollection was mistaken ('their
failure, which Mr Wordsworth ascribed to two causes, first the
Antient Mariner, which he said no one seemed to understand, and
secondly the unfavorable notice of most of the Reviews'),[287] anyway
on the second count. He thinks that the first reviewer 'blunders the
meaning and object' of several poems but is 'a man of talents and
learning'. The third review is 'so intelligent and so highly favorable,
as to read like an anticipation of this "milder day", when "these
monuments have all been overgrown".' ['Hart-Leap Well', ll. 175-6,
II, 254]. Field suggests that the first reviewer was William Taylor of
Norwich and the second Southey.

Field then mentions changes in *Lyrical Ballads* 1800, quotes briefly
from the *Monthly Review*, XXXVIII, June 1802, and again gives approvingly a long passage from the *British Critic*, XVII, February 1801.]

APPENDIX No. II *Extracts from the Poet's Pamphlet on the Convention
of Cintra.* [Field quotes two long passages from the pamphlet, without
comment: 'A people, whose government had been dissolved by
foreign tyranny, and which had been left to work out its salvation by
its own virtues, prayed for our help ... without being sullied or
polluted, pursue—exultingly and with song—a course which leads the
contemplative reason to the ocean of eternal love'; and 'Here let me
avow that I undertook this present labour as a serious duty. ... the
English army was made an instrument of injustice, and was dis-
honoured, in order that it might be hurried forward to uphold a cause
which could have no life but by justice and honour'.[288]]

APPENDIX No. III *A Quarrel of Authors.*[289] Mr Walter Savage
Landor, many years ago, published a poem called Gebir, in which there
is the following passage:—

---

[287] Quoted by Field from Cottle's *Early Recollections* ... in Chapter I. (Cottle
made a similar remark directly.) See n. 20.

[288] *Prose Works*, ed. W. Knight, 2 vols, London 1896, Vol. I, pp. 202-12, 223-33.

[289] De Selincourt, V, 428-9, and Moorman, *Later Years*, p. 592, give very brief
accounts of the supposed plagiarism.

But I have sinuous shells of pearly hue
Within, and they that lustre have imbibed
In the sun's palace-porch, where, when unyok'd,
His chariot-wheel stands midway in the wave.
Shake one and it awakens—then apply
Its polish'd lip to your attentive ear,
And it remembers its august abodes,
And murmurs as the ocean murmurs there.[290]

Mr Wordsworth's Excursion afterwards contained the following passage:—

I have seen
A curious child, who dwelt upon a tract
Of inland ground, applying to his ear
The convolutions of a smooth-lipp'd shell;
To which, in silence hush'd, his very soul
Listen'd intently; and his countenance soon
Brighten'd with joy; for murmurings from within
Were heard, sonorous cadences! whereby
To his belief the monitor expressed
Mysterious union with its native sea.

[Bk IV, ll. 1132-40, V, 145]

In the year 1836, Mr Landor printed a lampoon, called 'A Satire on Satirists, and Admonition to Detractors', in which he wrote, in allusion to these two passages:— 'It would have been honester and more decorous, if the writer of certain verses had mentioned from what bar he took his wine'. The Excursion was published in 1814. For more than twenty years, the want of acknowledgement of this imputed plagiarism had been [rankling?] in Mr Landor's mind. That gentleman was acquainted with Mr Wordsworth, through their common friend Mr Southey. There were other more recent mortifications of a domestic nature, on the part of Mr Landor, arising from 'the daily beauty' of Mr Wordsworth's life; but into these it were indelicate for us to enter. In 1836, out broke the Satire. It was all printed ready for distribution among Mr Landor's acquaintance. One of those, Mr Crabb Robinson had actually received his copy; when that friend not only of Mr Wordsworth and Mr Landor, but of all that have the good-fortune to be acquainted with him, persuaded Mr Landor to suppress the publication, on the score of want of originality, namely that the tattle it

[290] *Gebir*, Bk I, ll. 170-7, *Poetical Works*, Vol. I, p. 6. The poem was published in 1798.

contained, about Wordsworth's holding Southey cheap, had been anticipated by Lord Byron. Upon this ground Mr Robinson worked upon Mr Landor's pride to overmaster his spleen; and the many friends of Messrs Wordsworth and Southey were spared the pain of seeing this mischief-making between them and this slander upon both recorded in the pages of any more authoritative writer than the professed retailer of all such current gossip of the day, Lord Byron. This is only one, out of hundreds of such good-natured acts, on the part of Mr Robinson. Still Landor could never forget that he was, in his own conceit, the unpaid-for drawer of some of Mr Wordsworth's wine, and in [December] 1842, he contributed to Blackwood's Magazine a *new* 'Imaginary Conversation between Porson and Southey'—pulling to pieces all the prosaic and simple passages of Mr Wordsworth's poems, as the Edinburgh Review had done thirty years before. But too late; for these poems had now passed into classics, and were almost popular. The obsolete malevolence of this article needed no notice; but Mr Quillinan, the great poet's son-in-law, to his own honour, rather than to that of his revered relative (for he was above such shafts), in a subsequent number of Blackwood [April 1843], published a very able Imaginary Conversation between Mr Landor and the Editor of that Magazine from which I cannot deny myself the pleasure of transcribing the following complete refutation of this imputed plagiarism:—

'*North.* There is certainly much resemblance between the two passages ... the thought itself is as common as the seashell you describe, and, in all probability, at least as old as the deluge.

Landor. It is but justice to add that this passage has been the most admired of any in Mr Wordsworth's great poem.[291]

North. Hout, tout, man! The author of the Excursion could afford to spare you a thousand finer passages, and he would seem none the poorer. As to the imputed plagiarism, Wordsworth would no doubt have avowed it, had he been conscious that it was one ... It is in the application of the familiar image, that we recognise the master-hand of the poet. ... There is a pearl within Mr Wordsworth's shell, which is not to be found in your's, Mr Landor. He goes on:—

> Even such a shell the universe itself
> Is to the ear of Faith ...
>   subsisting at the heart
> Of endless agitation.
>
> [*The Excursion*, Bk IV, ll. 1141-7, V, 145]

[291] From Mr Landor *verbatim* [Quillinan's n.].

These are the lines of a poet, who not only stoops to pick up a shell . . .
[but looks] upon the ocean of things,

> From those imaginative heights that yield
> Far-stretching views into eternity.
> [*The Excursion*, Bk IV, ll. 1158-9, V, 147]'

. . . I cannot help wishing that Mr Wordsworth had taken his opportunity of deservedly complimenting Mr Landor's genius, as he did, in another instance, gracefully acknowledge Mr Montgomery's poem, entitled 'A Field Flower'[292]. . . . But I have admitted, in my Biographical Sketch, that one of Mr Wordsworth's few weaknesses was a disinclination to read and admire the works of his contemporaries.

It being well understood that Professor Wilson of Edinburgh ['Christopher North'] is the Editor of Blackwood's Magazine, and that gentleman being a poet of Mr Wordsworth's school, it may be asked, how come he to admit to publication Mr Landor's illiberal and stale paper. As long ago as in the year 1809, a letter, which is understood to be his, was published in Mr Coleridge's 'Friend', proclaiming himself, in enthusiastic terms, a disciple of Mr Wordsworth; and not many years afterwards, he came to live in the great poet's neighbourhood, and published his poems[293]. . . In the early numbers of Blackwood's Magazine, the subject of Wordsworth's poetry is taken up in a spirit of admiration and love, winged perhaps by a little Tory opposition to the Edinburgh Review. But in the same work may be also seen abuse of the same poet, both, as has been publickly asserted, proceeding from the same double pen.[294] It was therefore not surprising that both Mr Landor's and Mr Quillinan's Imaginary Dialogues should be inserted in the same work. I do not pretend to account for this conduct on the part of Mr Wordsworth's gifted neighbour and disciple. With the exception of Mr Southey and the Coleridges, father and son, the first of whom was a faultless person, and the two last, whatever their weaknesses, were always gentle and peaceable, Mr Wordsworth was

---

[292] See Wordsworth's 1807 published note, II, 490, on Montgomery; cf. comment on Landor's grudge, 'Sea-shells of many descriptions were common in the town [of Cockermouth]; and I was not a little surprised when I heard that Mr Landor had denounced me as a plagiarist from himself . . .' I.F. note, IV, 397-8, to 'Composed by the Sea-Shore', 1833. See also V, 428-9, and Moorman, *Later Years*, 592 and note.

[293] See the Friend of 14th December 1809 [BF]. Wilson was already in the district. See Moorman, *Later Years*, pp. 166-7.

[294] See Moorman, *Later Years*, pp. 299-300: 'Wilson's vanity had been offended when the critics sneered at his own poetry as a poor imitation of Wordsworth's . . .'

not fortunate in his neighbours. I have, in my text, adverted to the cases of Mr De Quincey and Mr Hazlitt. The motives of the Edinburgh Professor of Moral Philosophy are best known to himself. But perhaps if, in all Mr Wordsworth's seven volumes, a single whisper of 'Wilson' could be discovered, unquestionably a poet and a man of a most fertile critical genius, these things might not have been so.

APPENDIX

Two Letters from Field to Wordsworth

Liverpool, April 10. 1828.

My dear Sir,

Since you were kind enough to visit me here, I have been thinking of what you said concerning the several alterations of your Poems, which you made upon collecting them into 5 volumes; and I have gone through the long and instructive lesson of collating them all with the previous editions, correcting those editions with my pen, so as to shew the eye hereafter the various readings at a glance; and in performing this task, I have been amply repaid by both a deeper insight into the poet's meaning and a better lesson in the art of poetry, than I could have derived from any other sources. You will not be surprised at my having taken these pains, when you hear that *Ille ego qui quondam*—I am he who formerly completed in MS. interleaved in my copy of your 2 octavos, your Epistles from the Lakes and from the Alps and your Female Vagrant, which you may remember to have seen at our friend Charles Lamb's, thirteen years ago—such has always been my love for your poetry! These things being so, will you condescend, not now, but at your lesiure, to read a few remarks, the result of this collation?

And, first, I think I have detected a little disposition in your alterations, to mitigate that simplicity of speech, which you taught us was the true language of the heart, and to make some tardy sacrifice at the shrine of poetic diction; and thus, after having 'created the taste by which you have been enjoyed', in a small degree deserting your disciples. Why should Alice Fell and Andrew Jones have been omitted, or the Beggars and the Blind Highland Boy and the Gypsies altered, whether or not in deference to the utter want of sympathy of Mr Jeffrey or the conceit of Mr Hazlitt? I remember our friend Lamb quite agreed with me in disappointment with your substitution of the turtle-shell for the household tub (why should you fear to name it?) in which the Blind Highland boy launched himself on Loch Levin. To be sure, we thus gained that beautiful simile, 'Or as the wily sailors crept,' &c. But even this does not compensate me for the loss of truth, nature

and my washing-tub. I can't help thinking it very unlikely that the
sailors or the peasants of Loch Levin should not have sold the turtle-
shell to the comb-makers. But indulge me with your patience, if I go
regularly through such of your alterations as I think important, and
such as I shall certainly mark as 'Various Readings', if ever I have the
honour to be your Editor. 'The *fifteenth* Edition, with Notes by Barron
Field'. I presumed to tell you at Mr Littledale's, that I parted with the
identity of George Fisher, Charles Fleming and Reginald Shore, very
reluctantly for the sounding line [in 'Rural Architecture', I, 244]—

> From the meadows of Armath, on Thirlemere's wide shore;

but I thank you for the additional stanza: it moralizes: it is in harmony:
it is Johnsonian. It reminds me of what the Doctor said when Topham
Beauclerk and some other rakes called him up late one night: 'Well,
my lads, I'll have a frisk with you'. Your early epistles are greatly
altered and improved: they took me a deal of time to correct; but you
have struck out two lines [*Descr. Sketches*, 1793, ll. 790-1, I, 88], which
I used to think happy:—

> With cheeks o'erspread by smiles of baleful glow,
> On his pale horse shall fell Consumption go;

I hope not in deference to any small wit, who may have called this a
galloping Consumption.

> Where Discord stalks, dilating ev'ry hour
>
> [l. 800, I, 88]

reminds me of

> Discord! dire sister of the slaught'ring Pow'r,
> Small at her birth, but rising ev'ry hour!
> While scarce the skies her horrid head can bound,
> She stalks o'er earth and shakes the world around.

By the way, who is the author of these lines? [Garth: see following
letter]
    Ruth was always one of your most exquisite poems. I admit the
3 additional stanzas, beginning

> Sometimes most earnestly he said;

but I cannot prefer the alteration of

> And there, exulting in her wrongs   &c.

I feel that idea, and her 'carousing among her songs', much finer madness than being merely 'roused to fearful passion', which appears to me to be tame.

And now appears an illustration of my complaint of the loss of natural simplicity of language. In the Sailor's Mother, I greatly prefer the plain narrative,

> who many a day
> Sail'd on the seas; but he is dead,

to

> the waves might roar,
> He fear'd them not—a sailor gay.
> But he will cross the deep no more:

as I do

> Till he came back again

to

> And pipe its song in safety:

nor have I quite made up my mind, in the Emigrant Mother, to

> By those bewild'ring glances crost,
> In which the light of his are lost,

instead of

> For they confound me: as it is,
> I have forgot those smiles of his.

In the last of these alterations, the word *are* should be *is*; but for the harshness of *his is*; and so in the Idiot Boy, I would alter

> Has up upon the saddle set

to

> Has up *across* the saddle set,

and then say,

> *Over* the bridge that's in the dale.

And so again in Michael, I would read

> He went, and still look'd up *towards* the Sun,

instead of *up upon*.

Every alteration in Laodamia is a noble improvement. In the Green Linnet, one of my favourite quotations,

> A brother of the leaves he seems,

is taken from me, and I am fobbed off with

> A bird so like the dancing leaves.

In the 2d poem to the Celandine ['To the Same', II, 144], I am sure you will restore old Magellan, or even substitute Hippalus for Capt. Parry, when you come to reflect that you have coupled your navigator with the builder of the pyramids. In the 3d poem to the Daisy [IV, 67], I mourn the loss of the last stanza: to be sure, the moral is concluded with the 3d, but I think

> Thy function apostolical
> In peace fulfilling,

was a fine daring, and a most harmonious close.

As for the change in the Poem to a Skylark, I will not submit to it (I had almost call'd it—'flower stolen and coarse weed left'). The lark is no happy illustration of our 'hope for higher raptures, when life's day is done'; but his altitudes may console us in earthly pilgrimage. Altogether, I cannot part with such a line as

> With a soul as strong as a mountain River.

But the new poem to a Skylark is more perfect than all. Thank you for the 2 additional verses in the Wandering Jew. The idea of the clouds helmeting the hills is very happy; but we don't say 'a home *to enter*'. In illustration of your fine verses to the Cuckoo, let me tell you that it is of the nightingale that Lipsius says—'vox est, præterea nihil'. I have never seen the author of this common quotation pointed out before. I prefer

> At once far off and near

to

> As loud far off as near,

which is ambiguous, and may mean that the voice is heard as loud when coming from afar, whereas you mean that it is heard as loud by those afar off.

In the poem to the Nightingale you have in some degree disproved the charge I have the boldness to make against you, by restoring *fiery* for *ebullient*. In Goody Blake and Harry Gill, I think it made part of your case to state that

> In that country coals were dear;
> For they come far by wind and tide.

And now for the Gypsies. You were candid enough to admit to me,

in my delightful Sunday walk with you, that 'The stars have tasks, bu
these have none', should be restored. If so, this line must conclude the
Poem; and, pray, cancel that unnecessary apology

> Yet witness all that stirs,   &c.

'Beggars' is perhaps the strongest witness in support of my complaint

> A long drab-colour'd cloak she wore

is simple and natural; but her 'not claiming service from the hood o
a blue mantle' appears to me to be pedantic and artificial. The
substitution,

> Her suit no falt'ring scruples check'd,

seems to me to be a mere translation of the discarded passage into
poetic diction, such as you have justly reprobated in

> Turn on the prudent Ant thy heedless eyes.

And so of

> In their fraternal features I could trace   &c.

The reproof of looks, and the 'arbitrary and capricious expression'
'Heav'n hears that rash reply', could not have been very intelligible
to the two Boys.

In Yarrow Visited I think I trace the tasteful suggestion of our friend
Lamb that 'studious ease' had no business with the composition and
associations of the lovely picture.

In the Thorn, I humbly approve of the omission of

> I've measur'd it from side to side   &c.

In the poem of the Cuckoo, I am clearly for preferring

> Such within ourselves we hear
> Ofttimes—our's though sent from far;

and particularly the words

> Listen! ponder!

The verse of Young, which you want, in your fine lines on the Wye, is

> And half create the wond'rous world they see.

The line

> And kindle like a fire new-stirr'd

we discussed in our walk before-mentioned.

I acknowledge the valuable additions to the Address to Burns's Sons [III, 69]; and that Simon Lee is improved by patient and anxious alteration. The Force of Prayer has always been one of my prime favourites. Will you be pleased to accept with kindness the following Exposition of three of its finest stanzas?

'If for a Lover the Lady wept, she might melt into the River Wharf, tear after tear, exchanging the passion of love for that of death; and should this diversion of passion solace her, the same river that was death to her lover, would prove healing to her. Her love, which would then have been only sentiment and passion, might solace itself with the remembered image of her dead lover, and she might find a melancholy pleasure in plaining her woes to the ceaseless washing of the waters of the romantic river. Something to feed the fancy of the heart is all that a lover wants. But a mother's big heart, though wholly her husband's, and that whole buried in his grave, has ample room and verge enough for a long line of their son's posterity, and can enclose all the undeveloped involutions of that son's children's children. The genealogical tree of her son's promised posterity grew out of her buried husband's body: To her hopes, her son

was as a tree
Whose boughs did bend with fruit; till, in one night
A storm, a robbery,—call it what you will,—
Shook down his mellow hangings, nay his leaves,
And left him bare to weather.

In Peele Castle, the lines

The light that never was on sea or land,
The consecration and the poet's dream,

have passed into a quotation: they are *feræ naturæ* now; and I don't see what right you have to reclaim and clip the wings of the words and tame them thus:

The lustre known to neither sea nor land
But borrow'd from the youthful poet's dream.

The magnificent addition to the 2d Ode to Lycoris, I accept with gratitude.

But again, in Peter Bell, why, let me be permitted to ask, have you altered the homely beginning of a home-loving tale, the opening of which should essentially be homely, to contrast with the flights of the prologue?

The staff was rais'd to loftier height,
And the blows fell with heavier weight.

This seems to me a very laboured way of saying that Peter struck a poor beast harder than before.

> Like winds that lash the waves or smite
> The woods, autumnal foliage thinning,

sounds to me like mock-heroic, when applied to blows inflicted by a man upon an ass. Give me

> 'Tis come then to a pretty pass,
> But I will bang your bones.
>
> Quoth he, you little mulish dog.

Little strikes me as endearing: I would say *spiteful*. I remember once hearing a butcher describe the manner of feeding brawn, the whole process of fattening and killing which I believe is very cruel; and he said that while they were cramming the pig, it would kick, *it was so spiteful*. So would I make Peter call the ass *spiteful*. May I ask, why you omitted the stanza,

> Is it a party in a parlour, &c.

Of the omission of Peter's christianizing the cross upon the ass, I beg to approve, as it was a far-fetched idea.

I have now gone through your Miscellaneous Poems; and, hoping I have not quite exhausted your patience, will make a few observations on the Excursion. Here your alterations are many and judicious— principally abridgements—always improvements in the rhythm, the harmony and variety of which you have studied carefully.

> And make the *vessel* of the big round year

is to me ambiguous: by a vessel I at first understand a ship: I think the word *cup* would be more scriptural, as well as less ambiguous.

You say of the Solitary,

> for his mind
> Instinctively dispos'd him to retire
> To his own covert; *as a billow, heav'd*
> *Upon the beach rolls back into the sea,*

to any thing but solitude and a covert, back to the ocean of life!

> partook
> The bev'rage drawn from China's fragrant herb,

appears to me too much in the vein of Scriblerus. This is what I call poetic diction, in your bad sense: I would say,

> Merrily seated in a ring, drank tea.

To drink tea is too ordinary a practice now, to need any adaptation to the language of narrative blank verse, by wrapping it in classical or geographical diction.

My zealous admiration of your poems is the only apology I can offer to you, my dear Sir, for the exceeding freedom of these remarks. The candour, with which you did me the honour to converse with me, has brought them upon you. Although I have taken the liberty to put some of them in the way of questions, I have not the presumption to expect you will answer them. If you flatter me by adopting a few of the suggestions, and by forgiving the rest, it will be more than I deserve; and the favour of one short letter is all I can hope for, at your kindest leisure.

Did the Stage-Coach that bore you from Liverpool inspire you with any Sonnet, or was there nothing poetical in this docked town? Should you or any of your friends visit it again, I beg you will remember that I have removed to No. 8, Great George Square. Mrs Field desires to join me in kind remembrances to yourself and Miss Wordsworth; and in hopes that you will find Miss Dora, and bring her home, in restored health. I shall look wistfully over the sands, when I am at Lancaster Summer Assizes. The Duddon—the Duddon—I must see before I go abroad again; and it shall go hard but I will do myself the pleasure of calling upon you and Mr Southey.

My friend Mr Horace Smith wrote to me thus: 10th February last.

'I hope you told Mr Wordsworth that I was quite ashamed of the ridicule in the Rejected Addresses (not mine, by the bye)—that I had read his Excursion under my own walnut-trees with infinite delight; and had now the honour of being enrolled among his warm admirers. It must have been a high treat to you to go about with him.'

I will now put a period to this unconscionable Letter by subscribing myself,

> my dear Sir,
> > with the greatest respect,
> > > Your faithful humble Servant,

> > > Barron Field.

Address: William Wordsworth Esqr, Rydal Mount, Ambleside.

Liverpool, April 28, 1828.

My dear Sir,

Mrs Field begs you will offer her kind compliments to Mrs and Miss Wordsworth, as well as I mine; and we ardently hope that you will all cheer us on your way home, by resting a few nights with us . . .

Let me fill up my letter with thanks for your kind endurance of my poor sighs after the original readings, with which I first loved your poems, and my acquiescence, for the most part, in the reasonableness of your alterations. I accept the 'Beggars', as altered in your second Letter, as a noble improvement of all but the last stanza. 'I look'd reproof'. You say there is frowning, *shaking the head*, &c. Shaking the head is more than looking. Suppose you say 'I frown'd reproof'. You are so candid as to admit that 'Heav'n hears that rash reply', is too refined. What, if the poet spoke the first line to himself:

> Sweet boys! the heart shar'd not that lie.
> It was your mother, as I said,   &c.

and instead of '*joyous* Vagrants', in the last line, '*thoughtless* Vagrants'. I find that Dr Garth was the authour of 'Discord, dire sister' &c. But there is another Glee of Webbe's, with still nobler words, 'When winds breathe soft', of wch nobody knows the authour.

> *Over* the bridge that's in the dale ['The Idiot Boy']

occurs 3 lines after

> Has up *across* the saddle set   vol. i p. 226

> The silent heav'ns have goings-on—
> The stars have tasks—but these have none.

must be *all* retain'd, meo periculo. I like *goings-on*. It is mysterious—what *goings-on*, we know not—progress we know, but to what end, we know not.

I know you *meant* 'little mulish thing' in Peter Bell as contemptuous, but I contend that the word *little* is not contemptuous as applied to anything from which greatness is not expected.

> And make the *vessel* of the big round year,

you will find in the 9th book of the Excursion, towards the beginning.

I feel your argument as to the metaphor of the billow in the 5th book of the Excursion—that 'there is imagination in fastening solely upon one characteristic point of resemblance, stopping there, and thinking of nothing else'; 'the point simply is ⟨say you⟩ he was cast out of his *element*, and falls back into it, as naturally and as necessarily as a billow into the sea'. But the sea is not the *element* of a billow, at least in the popular meaning of the phrase *in and out of one's element*, though it be in the primitive meaning. However this is hypercriticism. I am satisfied with your defence, and thank you for the principle of taste, on which it is founded. In the beautiful history of the Quarrier and his wife in the 5th book of the Excursion, I think I have found a contradiction between that part of your account of the wife, in which you say,

> *In powers of mind,*
> In scale of culture, few among my flock,
> Hold lower rank than this sequester'd pair,

and that part in which you make her say,

> But above all, *my Thoughts* are my support.
> [Bk V, ll. 716-18, 823, V, 175, 179]

Let me not trouble you any more, but rather thank you for the improvements in the 'French Revolution', 'Simon Lee', and 'Rydale Chapel', which you have thrown in to me, 'more gaining than I ask'd'.

I have found the following particulars of the Countess of Winchelsea, if they shall be of any service to you . . . [Field here quotes from 'Memoirs of Learned Ladies', p. 432, and mentions a volume published by Lintot in 1717 which included poems by Lady Winchelsea.]

I thank you for your kind promise of showing me the Duddon. If it shall be convenient to you about the end of August, I propose to run over from Lancaster Assizes, across the sands, and either meet you at Coniston Water-head, or where you please.

Should you meet my brother at Trinity, remember me to him. He is rather deaf. Mrs Field begs to be always remembered to you. I gave your messages to Mrs Wordsworth and Mr Staniforth. And I am,

> my dear Sir,
> Your obliged friend and servant,
>
> Barron Field.

I was only anxious by my diluting Exposition of the essence-like text of the Force of Prayer, to prove whether I understood your meaning, and relish'd the spirit of that exquisite poem.

P.S. In the 4th book of the Excursion, I think it would read more intelligibly—

> From this infirmity of mortal kind
> Sorrow proceeds, which else were not; at least,

If Grief be something hallow'd and ordain'd,
And *in its due proportion* just and meet,
Through this *infirmity*, *it keeps* its hold
In that excess which Conscience disapproves.

[cf. Bk, IV, ll. 146-52, V, 113-14]

A little below [ll. 187-8], till you altered the word 'sleep' to 'rapt', I could not construe the passage, or make sense of 'craving' as applied to the dead. I used to transpose the lines 'Nor sleep' &c. and 'I cannot doubt' &c. and read 'Nor sleep, nor crave *they*' &c. Your alteration has solved all.

As you have elevated other prosaic lines in the Excursion and your other blank verse, let me recommend to the same *limæ labor*, the following line in the 4th book, near the end:

Accordingly, he by degrees perceives.

[l. 1218, V, 148] B.F.

Address: William Wordsworth, Esqr, Trinity Lodge, Cambridge.

AUSTRALIAN ACADEMY OF THE HUMANITIES

MONOGRAPHS

1 *Aspects of Celtic Literature*, containing B. K. Martin: *Old Irish Literature and European Antiquity*; and S. T. Knight: *The Nature of Early Welsh Poetry*, 1970
2 *Zagora 1, Excavation of a Geometric Settlement on the Island of Andros, Greece*, Alexander Cambitoglou, J. J. Coulton, Judy Birmingham and J. R. Green, 1971
3 *Barron Field's 'Memoirs of Wordsworth'*, Geoffrey Little, 1975

AUSTRALIAN HUMANITIES RESEARCH COUNCIL

MONOGRAPHS

1 *The Hopetoun Blunder*, J. A. La Nauze, 1957
2 *Mallarmé's 'L'Après-Midi d'un Faune'*, A. R. Chisholm, 1958
3 *Form and Meaning in Valéry's 'Le Cimetière marin'*, James R. Lawler, 1959
4 *The Art of E. M. Forster*, H. J. Oliver, 1960 (out of print)
5 *Bandello and the 'Heptaméron'*, K. H. Hartley, 1960
6 *Walter Pater*, R. V. Johnson, 1961
7 *The Melbourne Livy*, K. V. Sinclair, 1961
8 *Essays in Mycenaean and Homeric Greek*, G. P. Shipp, 1961
9 *The Thesis of 'Paradise Lost'*, G. A. Wilkes, 1961 (reprint 1968)
10 *The Similes of the 'Iliad' and the 'Odyssey' Compared*, D. J. N. Lee, 1964 (out of print)
11 *'Double Profit' in 'Macbeth'*, H. L. Rogers, 1965
12 *The Enragés: Socialists of the French Revolution?*, R. B. Rose, 1965 (reprint 1968)
13 *Aldous Huxley and French Literature*, Derek P. Scales, 1969
14 *The Structure of Sir Thomas Malory's Arthuriad*, Stephen Knight, 1969 (reprint 1974)
15 *André Gide and the 'Roman d'Aventure'*, Kevin O'Neill, 1969